SIGNAL DECAY

SIGNAL DECAY

JAY SNODGRASS

HYSTERICAL PRESS

Design, production: Jay Snodgrass
Type Styles: Acumin Pro
Library of Congress Cataloging-in-Publication Data
Signal Decay
by Jay Snodgrass — First Edition
ISBN — 978-1530047376
Library of Congress Cataloging Card Number — 2016902589

For personal orders, catalogs, and information, write to:

HYSTERICAL BOOKS
1506 Wekewa Nene • Tallahassee, Florida 32301
hystericalbooks@gmail.com
Published in the United States by Hysterical Books
Tallahassee, Florida • First Edition, 2013

Special thanks to THE THOMASVILLE CENTER FOR THE ARTS for providing
me with a residency at Studio 209, without which this would not have been
possible.

Thanks to Kristine, Abby, Darlene, Maria, Rachel, Emily A, Emily E, Karen,
Caprice, and all the staff at TCA. Also thanks to Southern Regional Technical
College, all my fellow faculty and staff, you also made this possible.

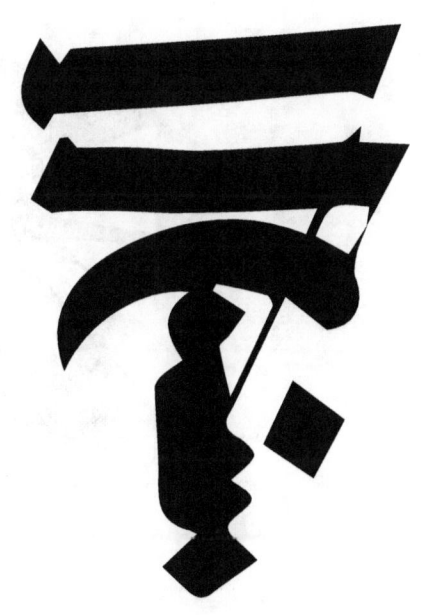

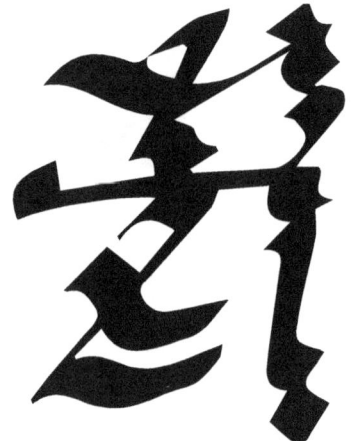

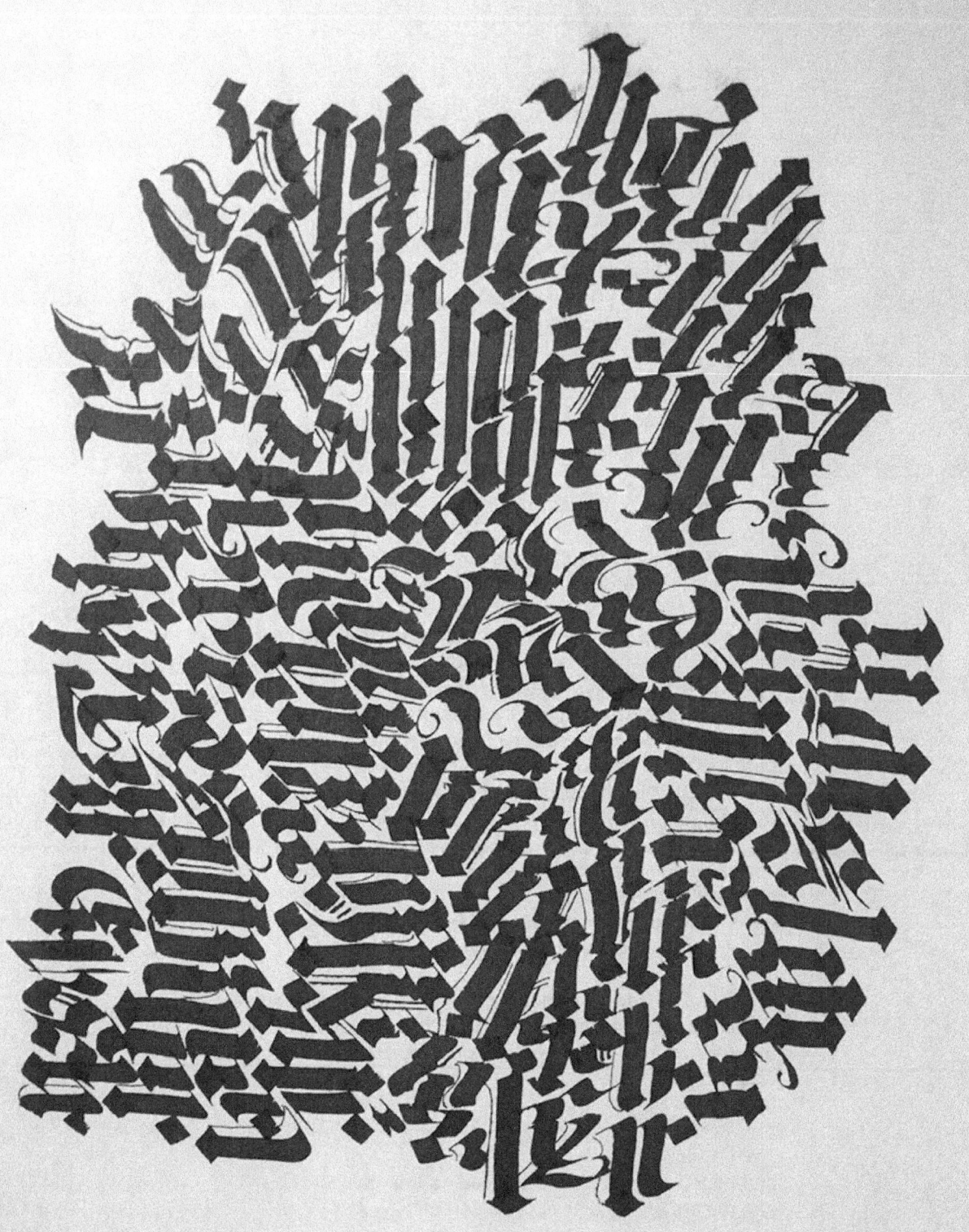

I threw a rock from the top of a mountain
covered in cloud mist and airy fingerprints.
I couldn't see and so had no mind, there was only
the gray vapor, a limitless nothing, nothing beyond my
fingerprints. I found a rock at the top of that mountain,
and it was round smoothed from air, eroded
by water's fingers rubbing.

The foot of the statue of Saint Ugolino,
Saint of fallen structures, has been rubbed raw
by devouts and pilgrims, driven by vision, wanderers,
blind to meaning, led by their fingers,
the cloud's wet braille,
so that now visitors are forbidden
to touch the stone,
forbidden to leave their finger's grease
to pool in the stone's microscopic recesses.

I threw a stone from the mountain because the clouds obscured
my vision. I had no sense of a world beyond me.
I lived in a casement of gray, of anger,
of unfathomable language. I lived inside the desire to speak
and make smooth the jagged precious stones of order,
hard like the crystals of ice in the cold enclave
of a tumbled childhood, desolate, bruised
by the heavy hand on dark centuries of children.

I have inside me a thousand years of wind, of wailing
choked through a chasm;
because inside me there was nothing, I threw the rock at the vapors,
and it went out and away from me.

When I came down the mountain, a girl was unconscious,
hit on the head by a stray rock. Had I seen anyone
throw a rock from the mountain top? No, it wasn't me,
wasn't meant to be
that.

Thing is down here the sun is shining
and the concerned faces are receding from me
into the groups I will never be a part of.

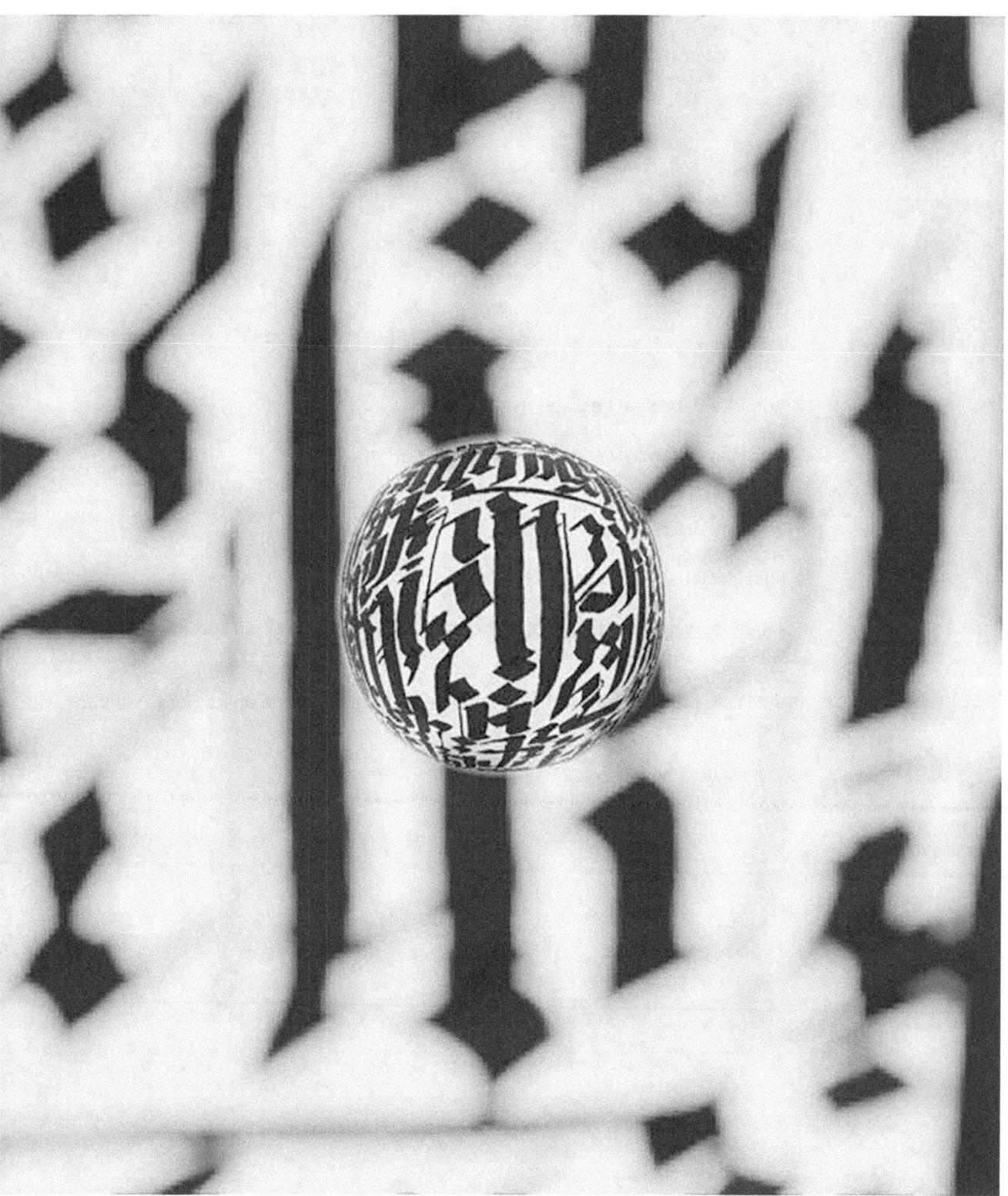

Admire what doesn't escape
like breath
whistling as the pipe constricts,
raising the note

Bequeathed somber constancies,
vigorously poised
on dark stones

I want to go up I want to go up I am wax. I am wax. You give me wax. Molded. I am
wax.
Molded by hands
until I am solid I want to come apart to decay. I cannot come apart. Solid I want to
decay

Will I always be this cold?

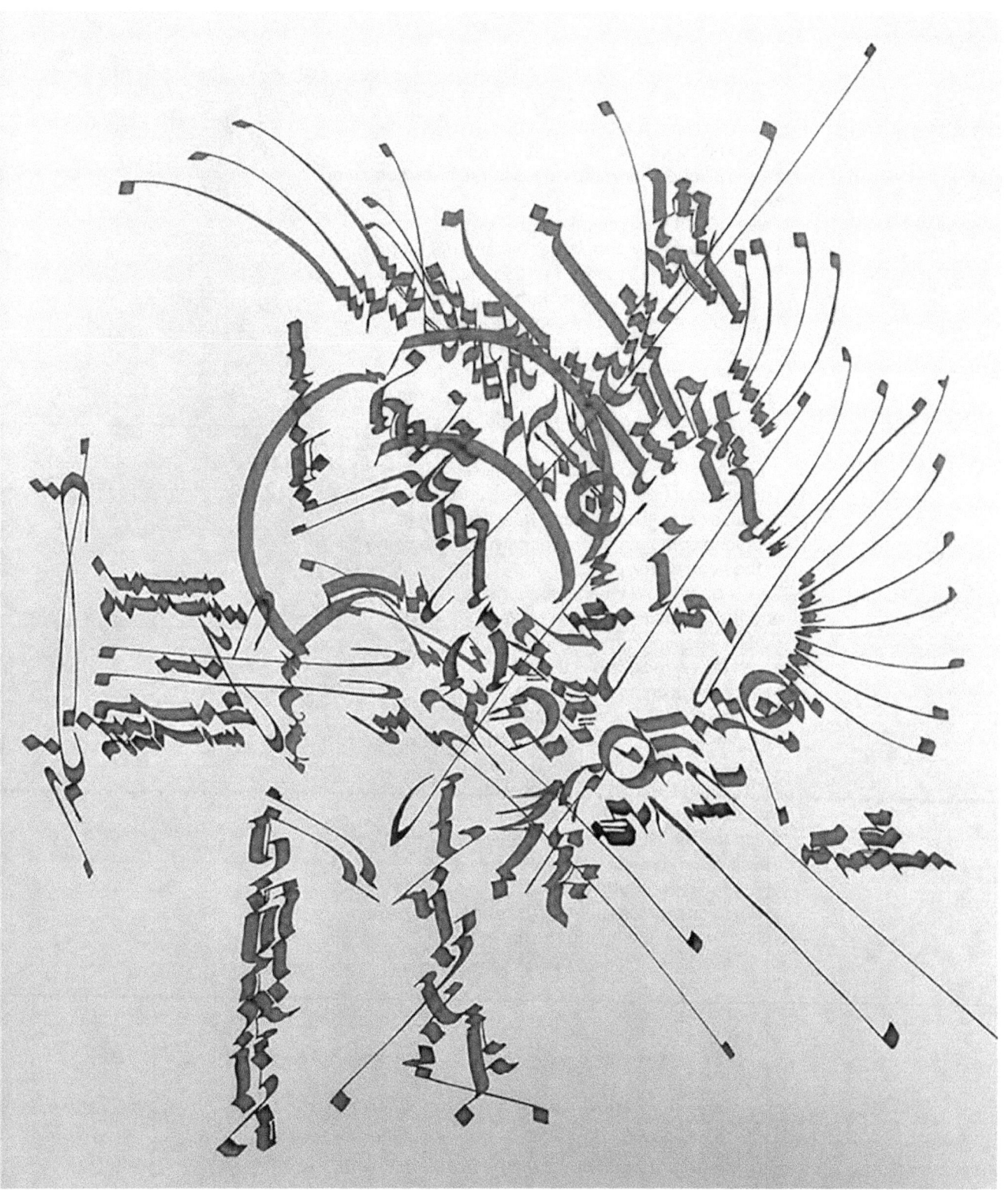

This is all about the time I threw rocks.
This is all about how the bones in the back don't work
after a while.
This is about the time I threw rocks.
This is about how people get old and die (boring).
This is about the time I felt bad for hitting
a girl in the head with a rock that I threw.
This is about feeling sad about nice weather.
This is about not being able to play baseball
because I was afraid of being hit in the head.
This is about being hit in the head with a rock.
This is about being hit with a head.
This is about how when you love something really cute
it dies and then it's not cute anymore.
This is about how people tell me things
because I'm a "listener" and how listening to
everyone complain about their lives is like being hit
in the head with a rock.
This is about how when people get sick
and they complain but don't listen
that is like being a rock. This is
about how a rock that is thrown listens
to where it is going. This is about how
the ear can be filled with water. This is
about how rocks lie along the bottom of a river
and can hit you without even moving.
This is about jumping in to the water
to not have to listen to your complaining
anymore and hitting my head on a rock.
This is about how blood slips away
along the current and doesn't really
seem to change anything. This is about
splitting open and letting the rocks fall
out. This is about falling open this is about

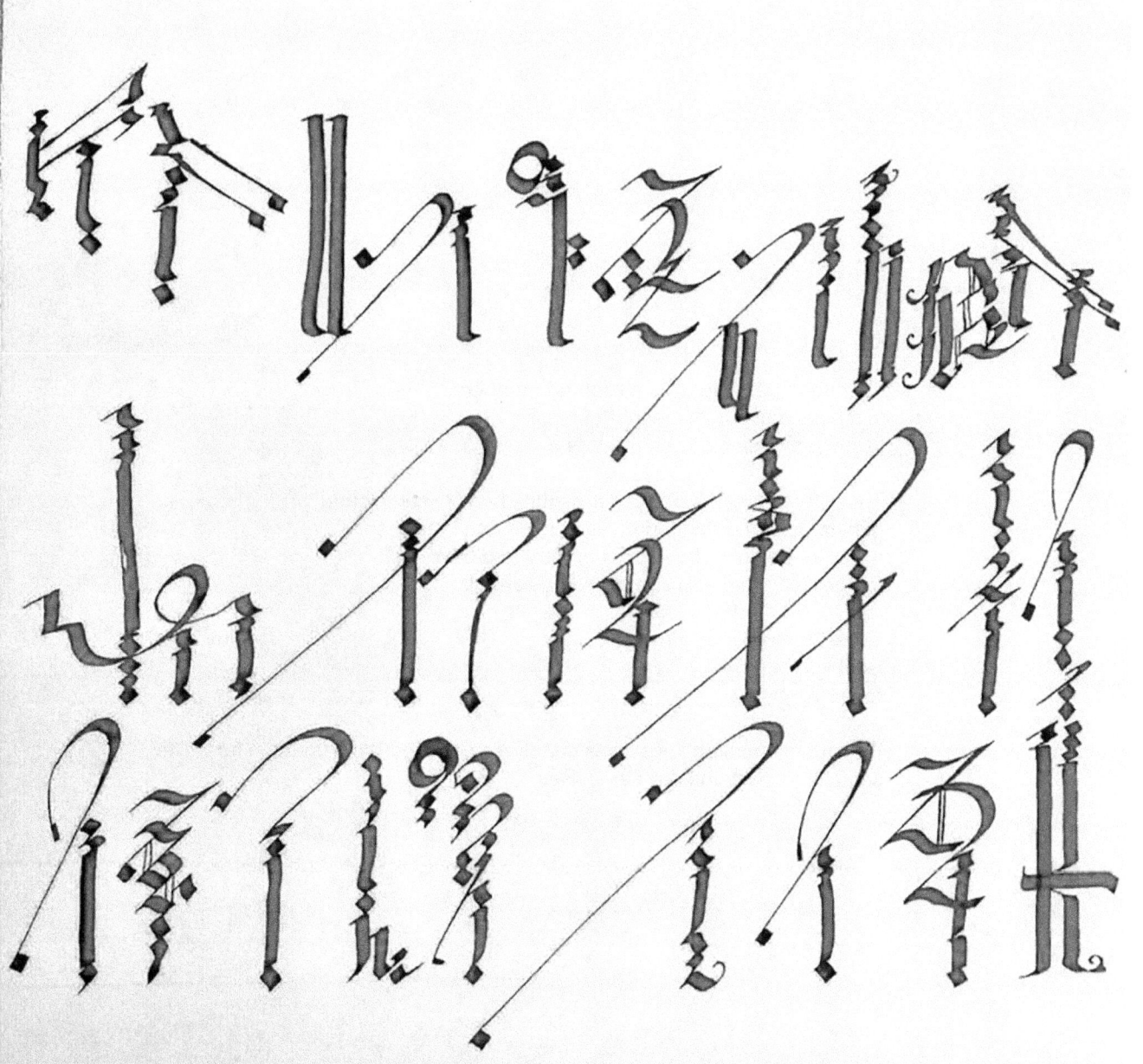

Nutrition's painting   throbbing numbers
semblance of odium, delightful masks
listen to the alien colors, the forest

These trees breathe up your mosquito poison, car's tears,
generations of forbidden miles that we don't really care
about as we soar above our depression, above
the ground the blackness sucked us out of.

These trees give us form, give way,
leaving echoes
to fall in.

What holds nothing in its arms can fly, so can drag the serpent in its claws,
scratching away the days as it rises.

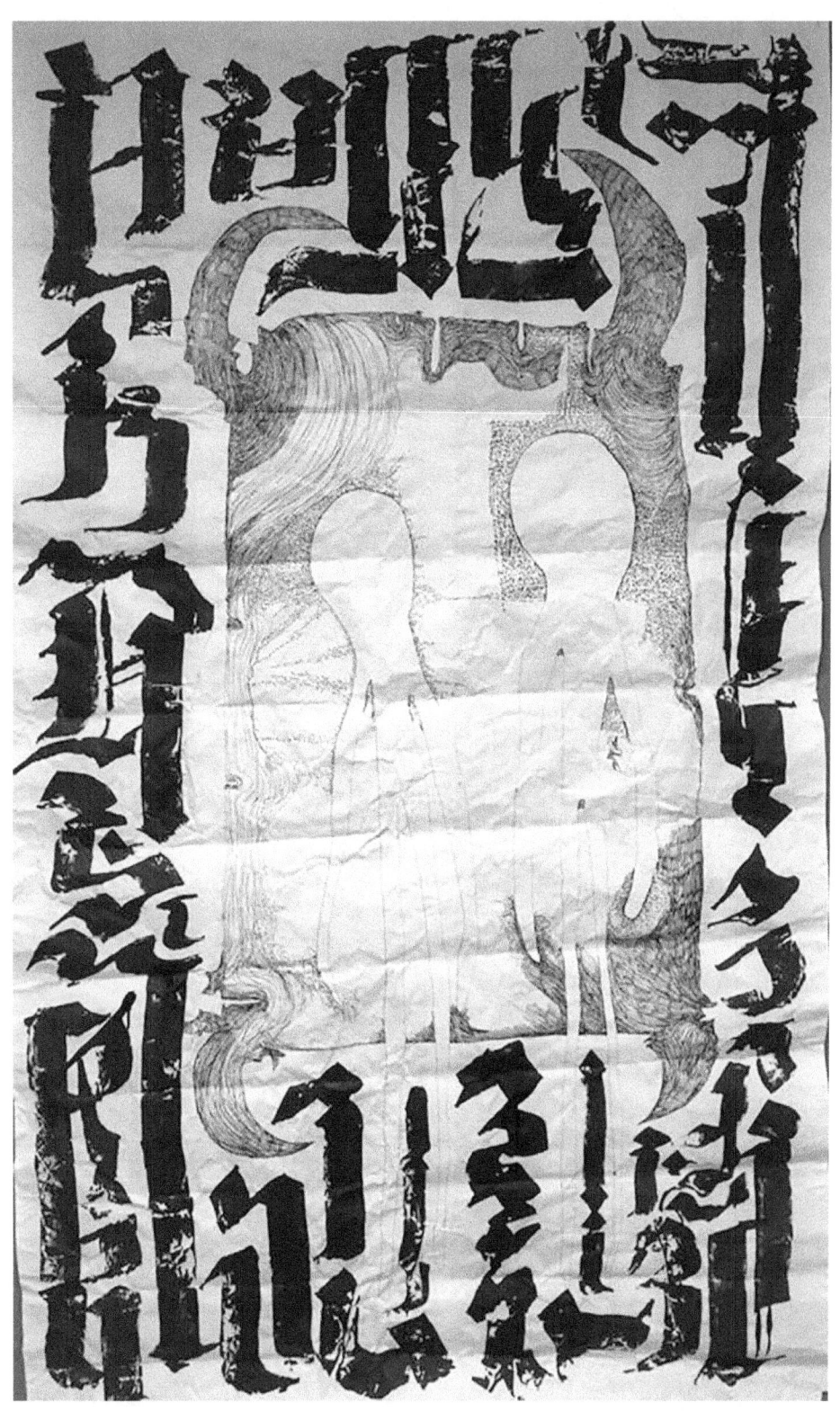

Turn toward the sound,
                             cloud scarred sky,

turn from the spot, carrying coffee in a paper cup, look
across a bridge, through the mist, a woman,
then she is obscured.

She is following the current of her days, the sound of it,

the centipede's many legs stepping on heaven, pulling its body half in through
the cracks, finding nothing, then reversing.

In the barest rectangle, you formulate high ceilings
through the clustered dusk, and the furniture like mute children
lurks.

The children in the paintings are blind, each eye a portal/petal
through which shades travel to the polished world.

The leaf folds over and dies when it is time, not when the air drops.

The connection between us is not error,
it is the season of light which transforms.

With luck you may survive the doctor's eye,
you may see the formula of moving air
dynamic, full of the fever of thought

Shredded, the desert birds flutter to fabric
swab the soul in farewells, ill-spoken

The talkers grow weary of our listening. The lake doesn't hear the frog, but carries
the voice as it immerses, folds of gold light and green.

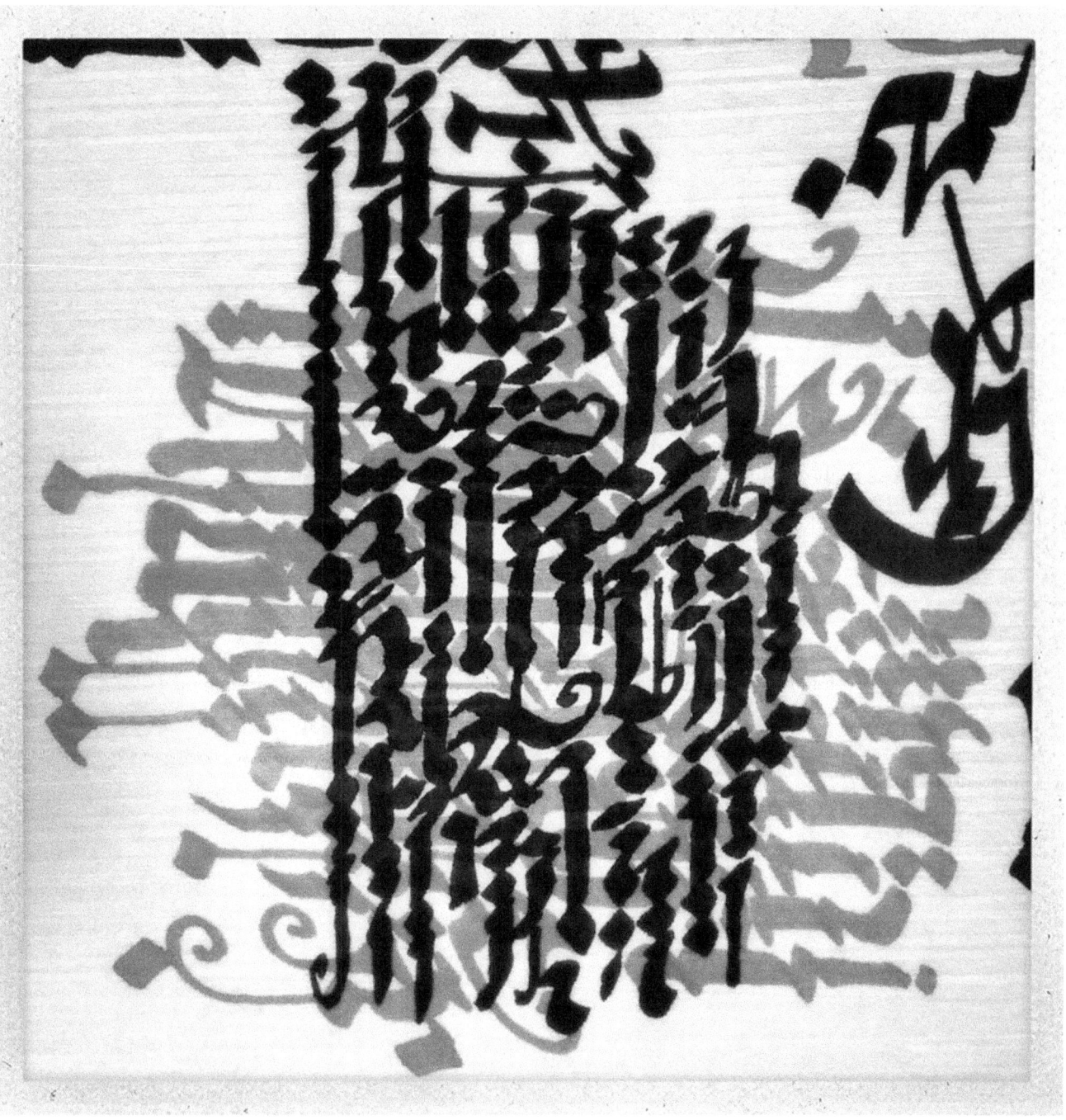

The family pet, ecstatics, is prone to commune with spirits
and be possessed, then forced for weeks to recover from
its spiritual outburst.

A hyper inactivity, retuning.

These gashes are infinite, bones turned to stone
through the process of weeping, my calcified days/eyes.

I never want to forget, which is why I can't sleep. The ginkgo tree in the parking
lot keeps its leaves far too long, holding on to the evening's street lamp.

Keepsake, the humbled one, profile of G.....
the ridge beyond the passing rise, too fast
the dreadful password.

Look away, the signs speak in garbled waves.
We nod convulsively as passengers on a boat
are turned to the wave's indication, the space between
reading and sign is decay:

Where are you? Lost as the bridge forgets the river it spans.

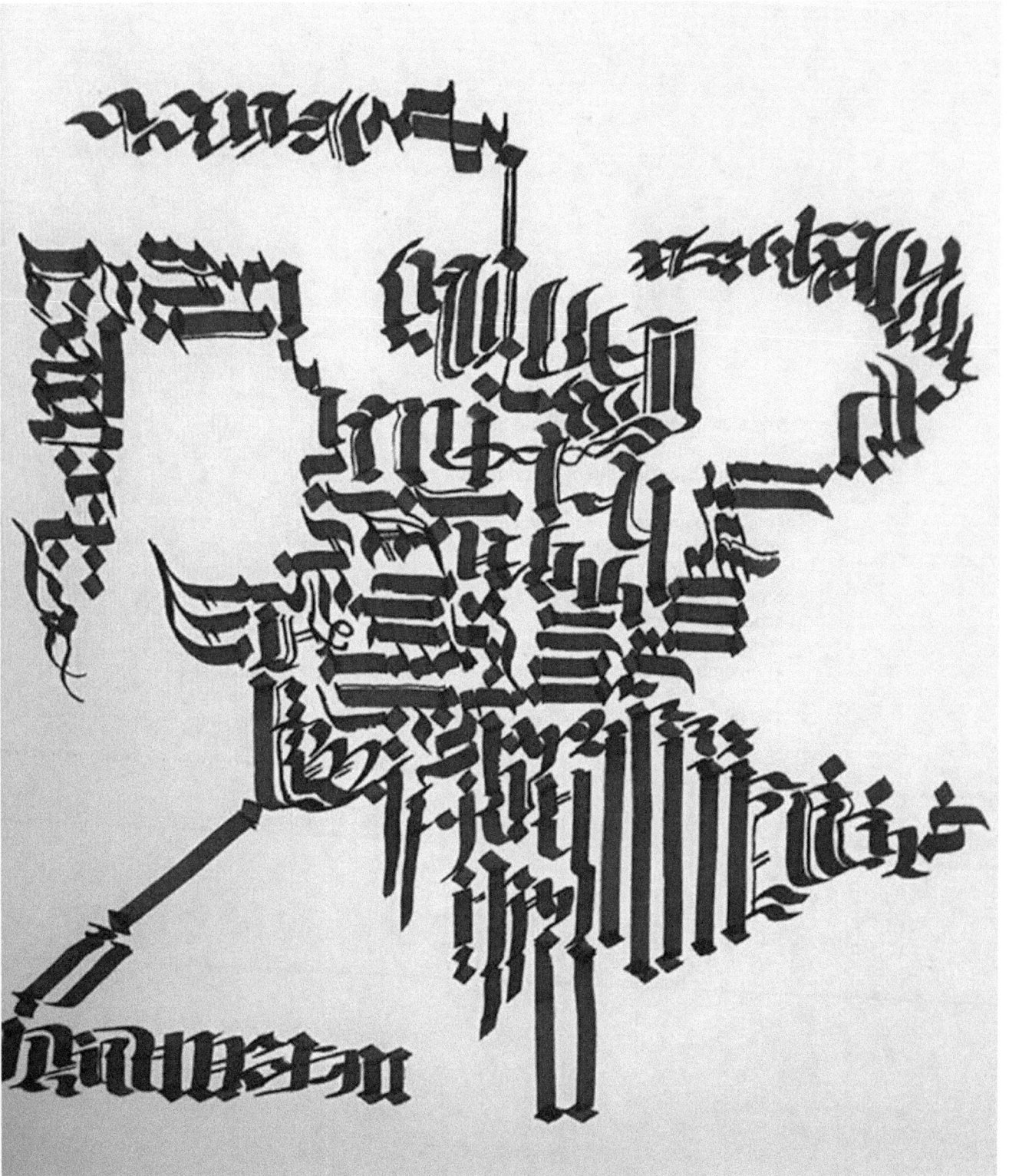

The sign scatters light, pushing back.

A stone lies beside the river, it does not call.

I pick it up anyway and throw it just to see
something break open.

Smile at your most desolate flower,
scoured by dreams.

The bombs fall to us wanting to share the loneliness of explosion.

The thing we do well together, expand so quickly there's nothing left.

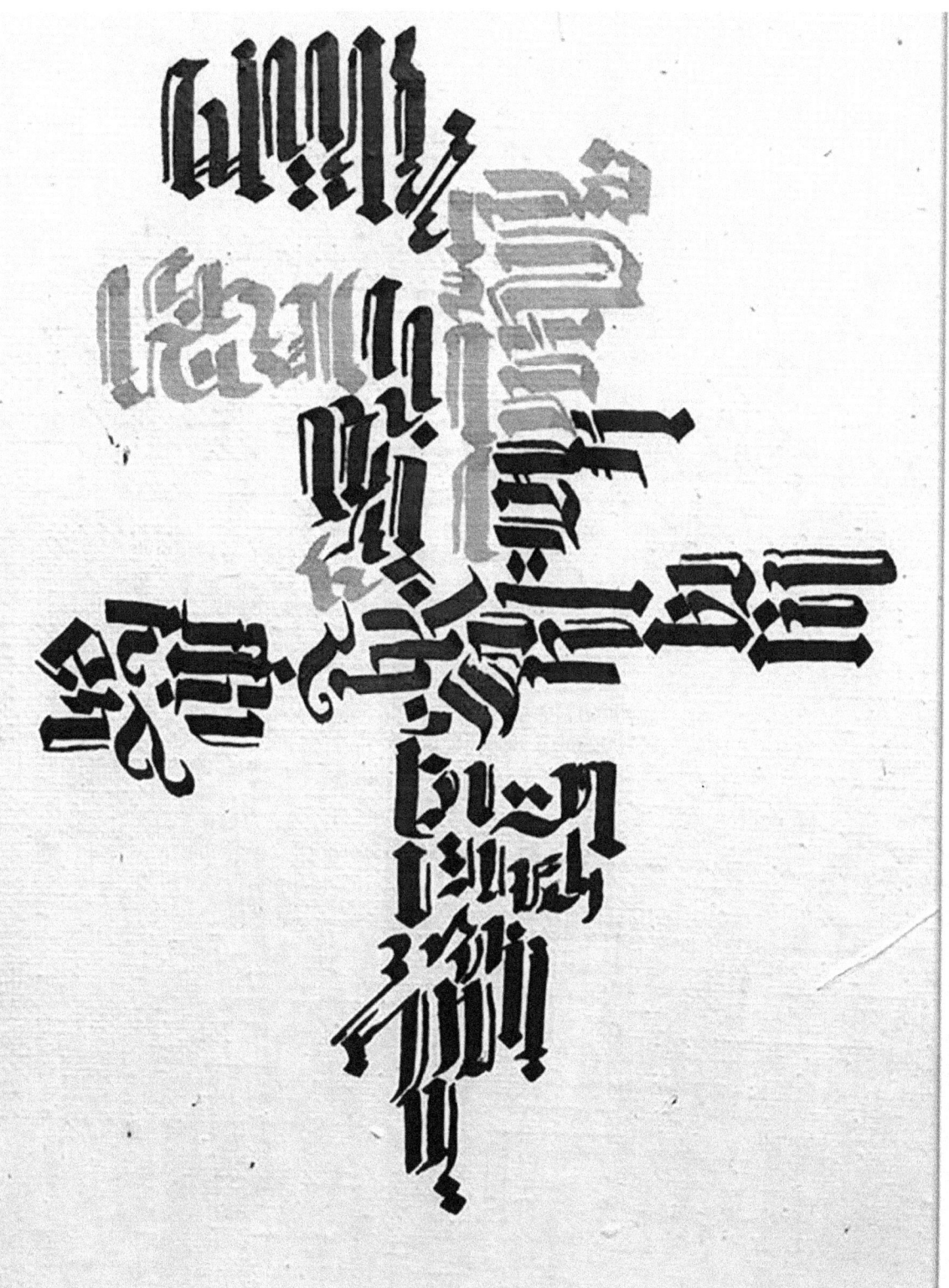

27

Stand up straight, polish your skeleton
        to a smooth stone,

        powder affirms itself
in sleepless fumes.

The televisions looks back
            as we are preparing to die,
and the the sacrifices we make to the wall-clock, cuckoo tock
            and the sofa
                    is as rigorous
                    as any sainted suffrage.

        As the signal shuts down,
            salute
the cold triangle of Earth's first satellite
leaving the solar system,

        give out a low moan.

        It is the sound I am receiving.

Sky so heavy.

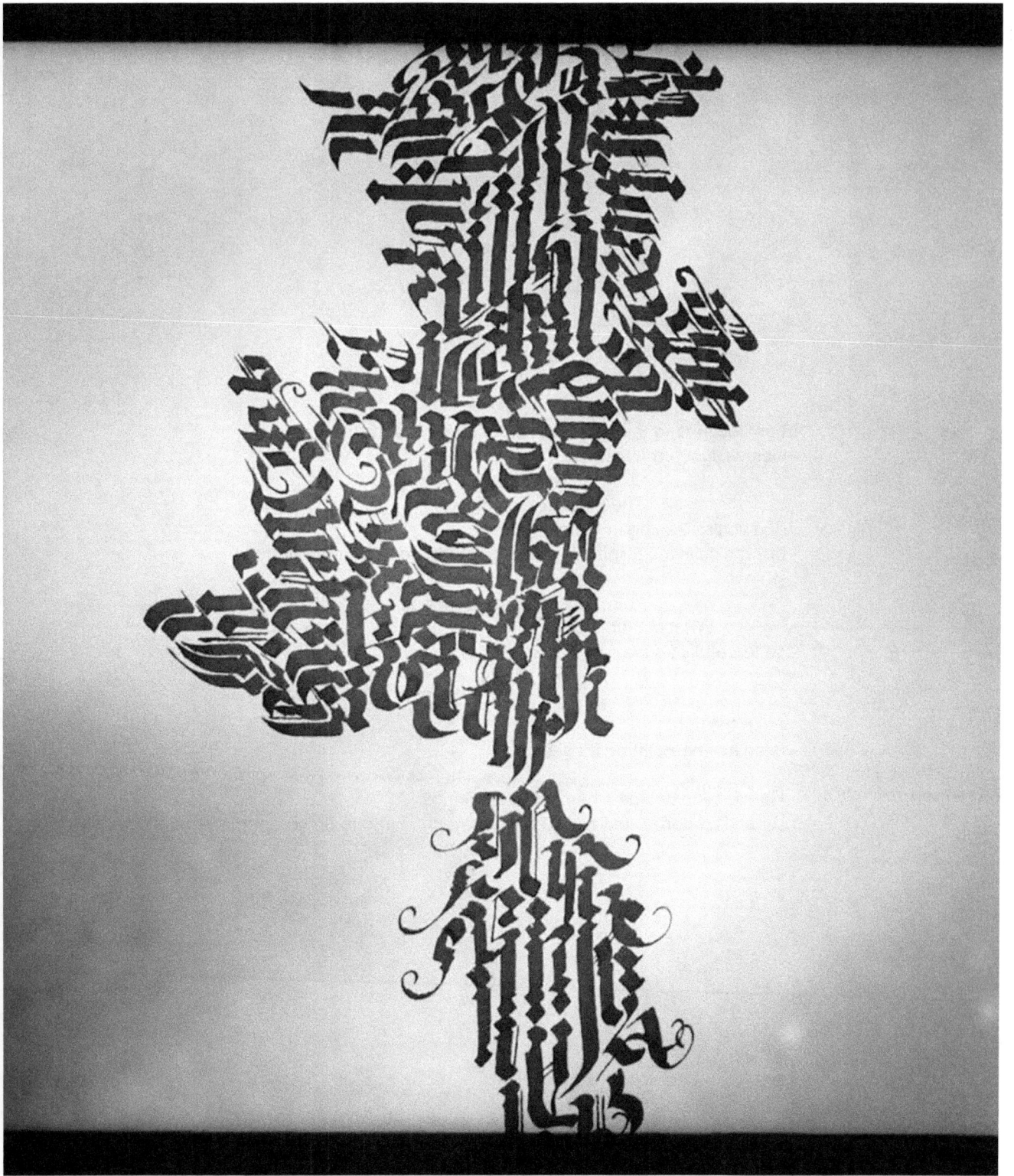

I am inclined to the sounds of cruel music, nocturnal,
vicious. Nocturnal, remiss.

                The cruel joke
of it you're leaning in to hear
but the cells are turning inside out, snapping in horrid rhythm.

                Your naked shame is inconclusive.
           What should it be,
so forcefully squeezed
                      into words.

Even the light
is on its knees, lifting a hand.

How do you decide when to stop looking?
When is it done? Just as you turn away, choosing to do so, so this work is abandoned.

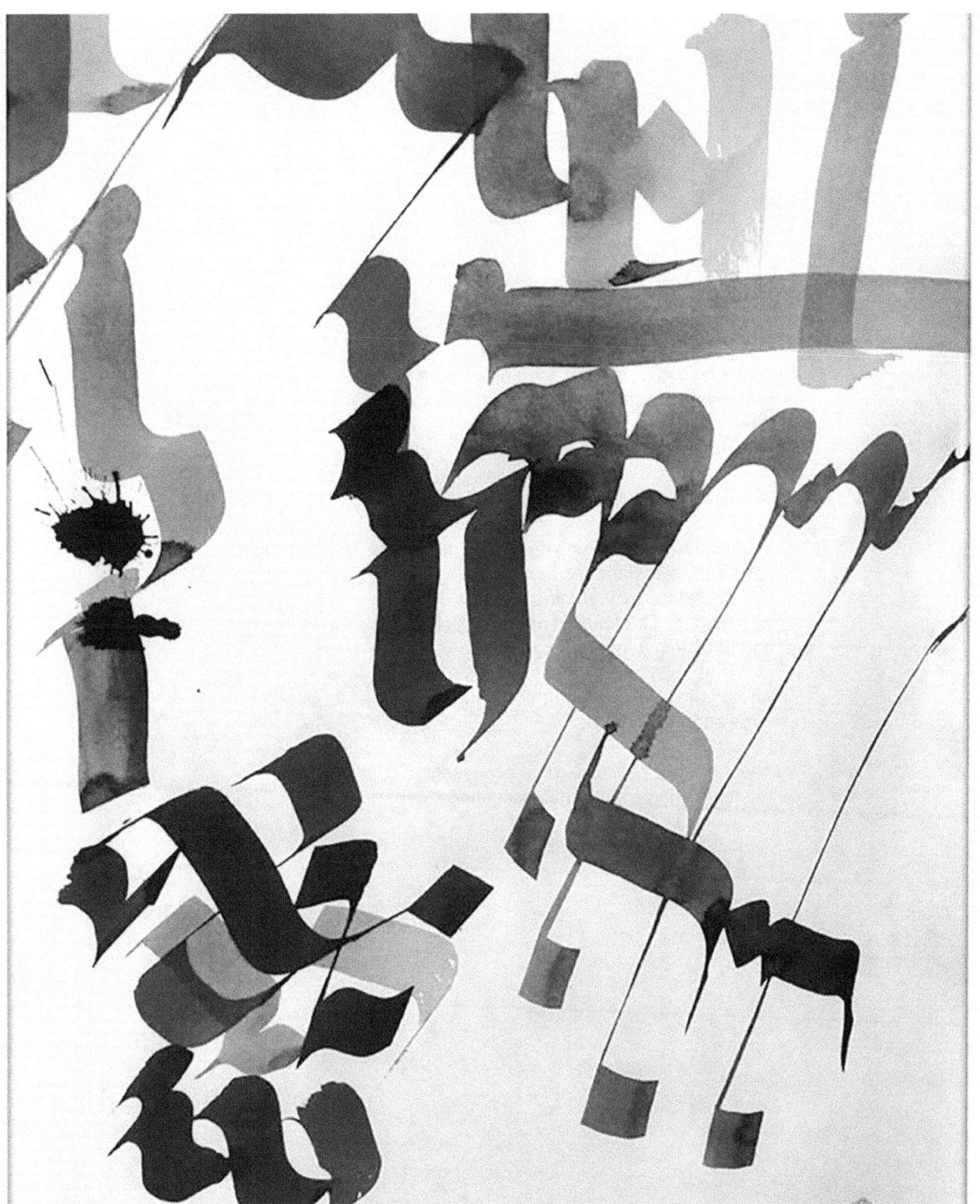

Single bulb love, radiant, singing *no-halo*,
as beneath we sing no breath,

flinging from half shadow to half being the light,

our own flickering, fades just as quick.

Meanwhile, evening runs its fingers across the forest's braille,
soft freckles, melanomic bumps,
and the saints are watching, mouths dry,
watching me lift meaning off the dirty floor
and put it in my mouth.

And on the gentle rise on the road to your alabaster heart,
birds and trees leak out.

A water tower rises like a rite of passage,
the town's name marked *Consequence*.

A most beautiful turning away.

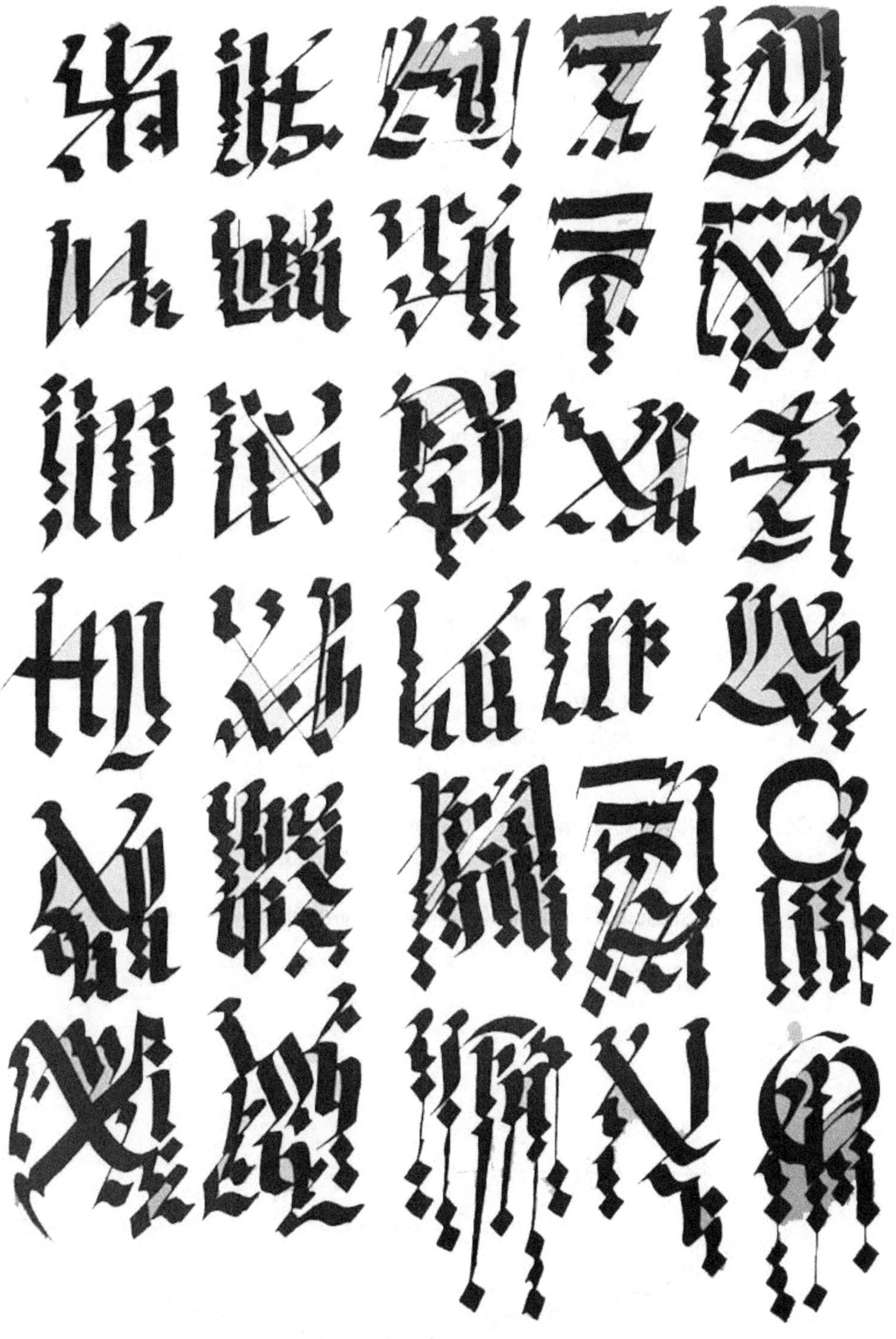

You may, in the dark wood, touch a tree
in hopes the texture will spark some long
unremembered note, a triggering roughness,

you may hope to bond with, be clutched by
and absorbed into the fiber.

                You may pull
                away to find it is only night again.

Excavate a coat of butterflies,
        a riderless horse, saddled in jewels,
            I will give away my shoes and walk in the wet grass.

Cold and gray rain on the window may be
            the most comfortable kind of death.

      Trust the ancestors to help decide what the paintings on the cave wall

                                show.

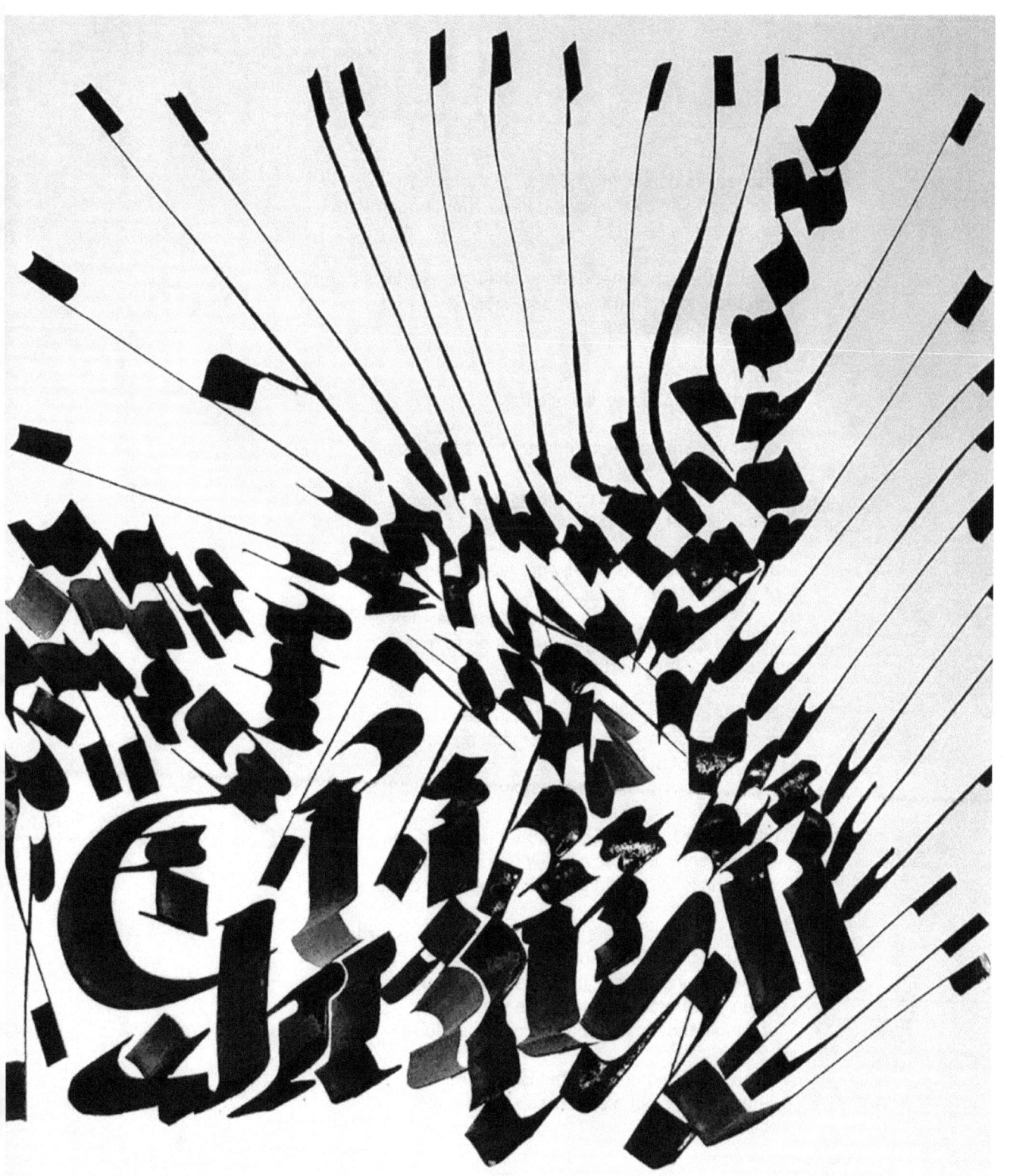

35

Sunflowers bob as in worship.
I am confused by the reeling birds, their judgements
submitted as results:

I watch the light deteriorate to shadow, as after a bomb,
and the crickets sing like doors closing
on an emptied closet.

Watch the light swallowed.
Watch the stone rise like a leaf,

the stone is not a heart, it is not hurled, the stone

that isn't hurled does not want the blood
to come from your head when it strikes,
                                        it feels
bad after rising like a leaf, after feeling the current
of air billow like a dress,
                        it feels like it has a heart
as it dips, the drop of gravity enough to make
a space for the heart to live in,
                                it drops
into the cavity which is not the space of the heart
but which is the space of another's brain,
the center of being,
                        and the stone that isn't a heart
makes a turn for the worse, turn for the better,
hits hair and skin and bone and blood and lust
and hunger and turns away with a red mark
where its heart would be, red for rage, for bursting,

for tears and ricochets and ringtones and discarded
cracks of thought, of sound of concrete, cracks
in the day, in the light, in the thoughts you had
when you were creased across the temple,
praying hands reach up to receive the blood,

come away with a lump that is not a heart,
a heart that is not a stone, a sound, a crazy
sound I said.

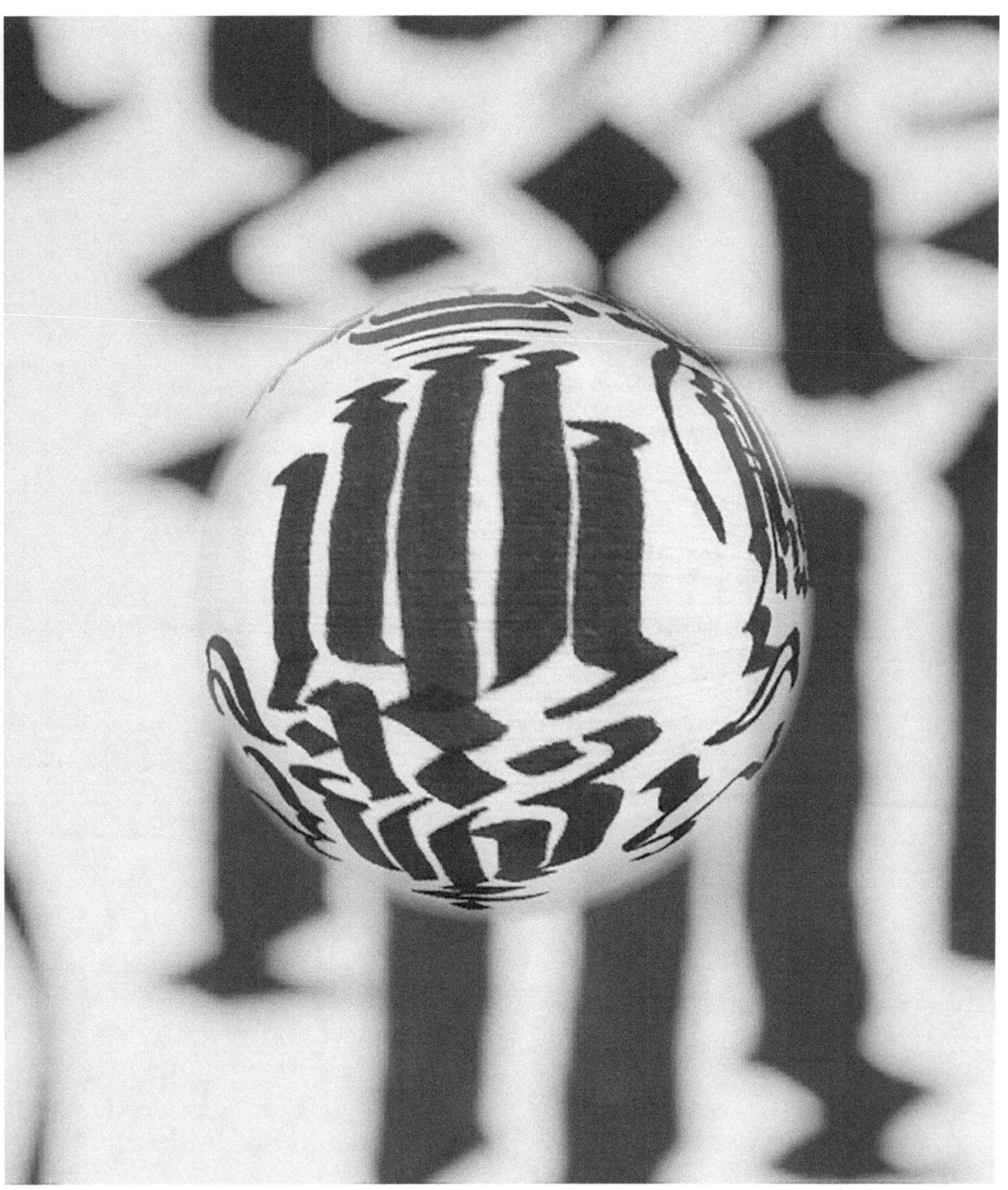

Radio signals dip into cloud depressions,
                                    may be lost.
We cover the windows against debris,
                              yard items
become missile.

              The pin-hole camera accumulates
enough light to stain a film with shadows.

We sit through the outage around candles, flickering
our faces for something to say, anything to protrude.

Seeing through the dark glass into your photograph, I am torn out, thorn-out,
throughout, thorn, you, daughter unknown
in glass, your long hair, like a window, destroys me.

Listen the eye of the storm, hammering like a train.
I am the railroad spike poised at the tie,
the sun is the hammer
and the days are the driving wail
dropping from a song.

Dial tone, I offer this a once over, once and for all.

And memory speaks in chips like glass, giving me enough
revelation to invent myself out of the mowings of
my past.
     I know there was a book here, with a red spine
and black letters, maybe it was azalea you were standing next to
when you told me,
         dark shadow of midday beneath around your feet.

     Here is news: here are trees,
              the persistent sun
    chews at your face, demanding:
            take me in your hands,
    punctuation is in order,
          order is the cutting of hair.

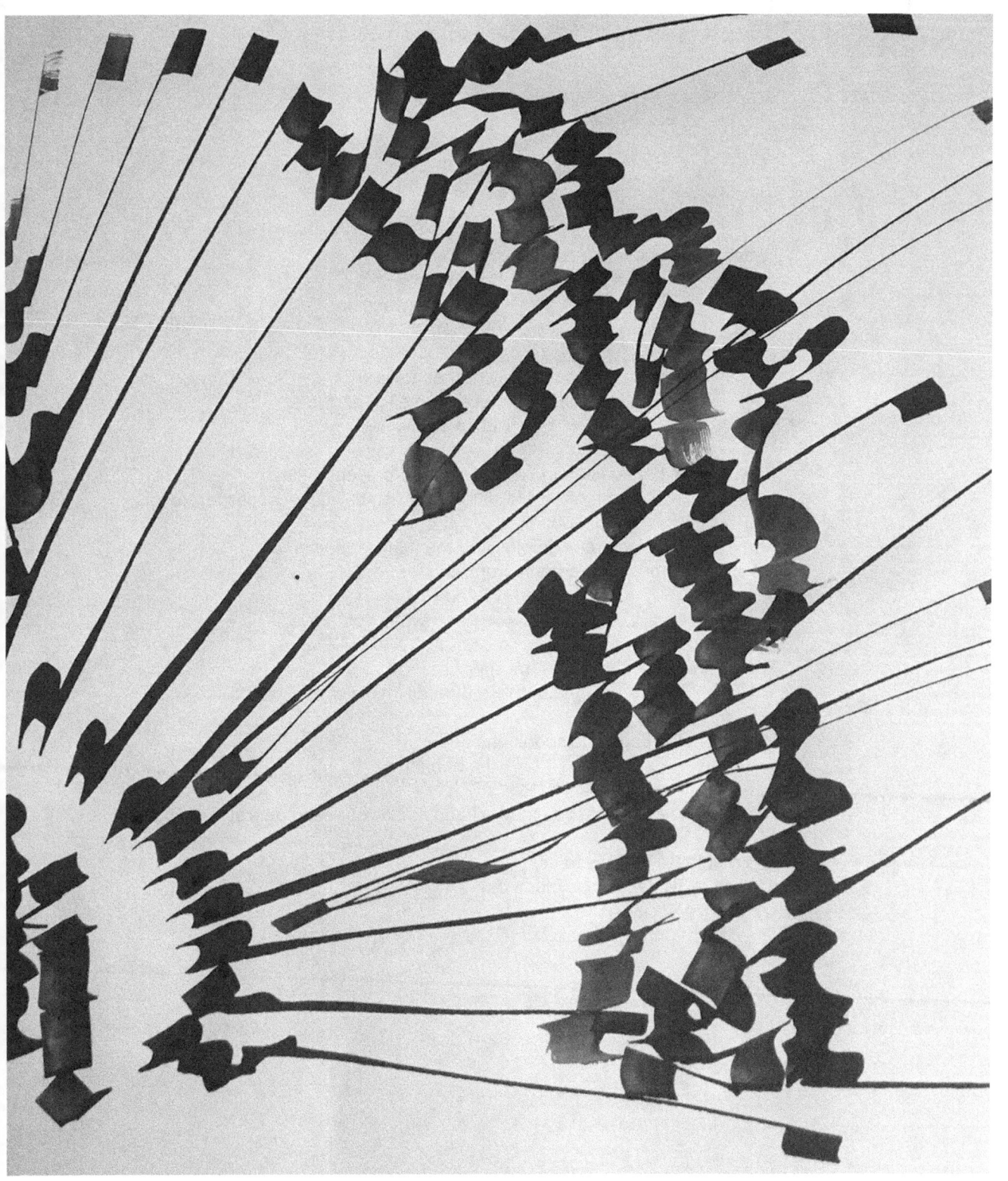

I want you to know you can't trust me
                              to say
                              when you wake up
it will not be over.

          And we could go this way or that, towards
                    a breakfast joint, or the smell of perfume
                              in an empty hallway.

To where the breakfast menu is laminated to prevent decay,
                    and it offers the different schemes you were desperate for.

And the smell is cigarette smoke, and the things it points to
are still just around the corner, promising
                              to be revealed
                                        when you arrive.

Promising to sew the rips in the sky
                              with these threads, these careful words

fallen from the page and spooking
                                        the horses.

I want you to know that you may fall and strike your head on a stone,

and that these leafless trees,
goaded by winter, will be plumed
with light and sky.

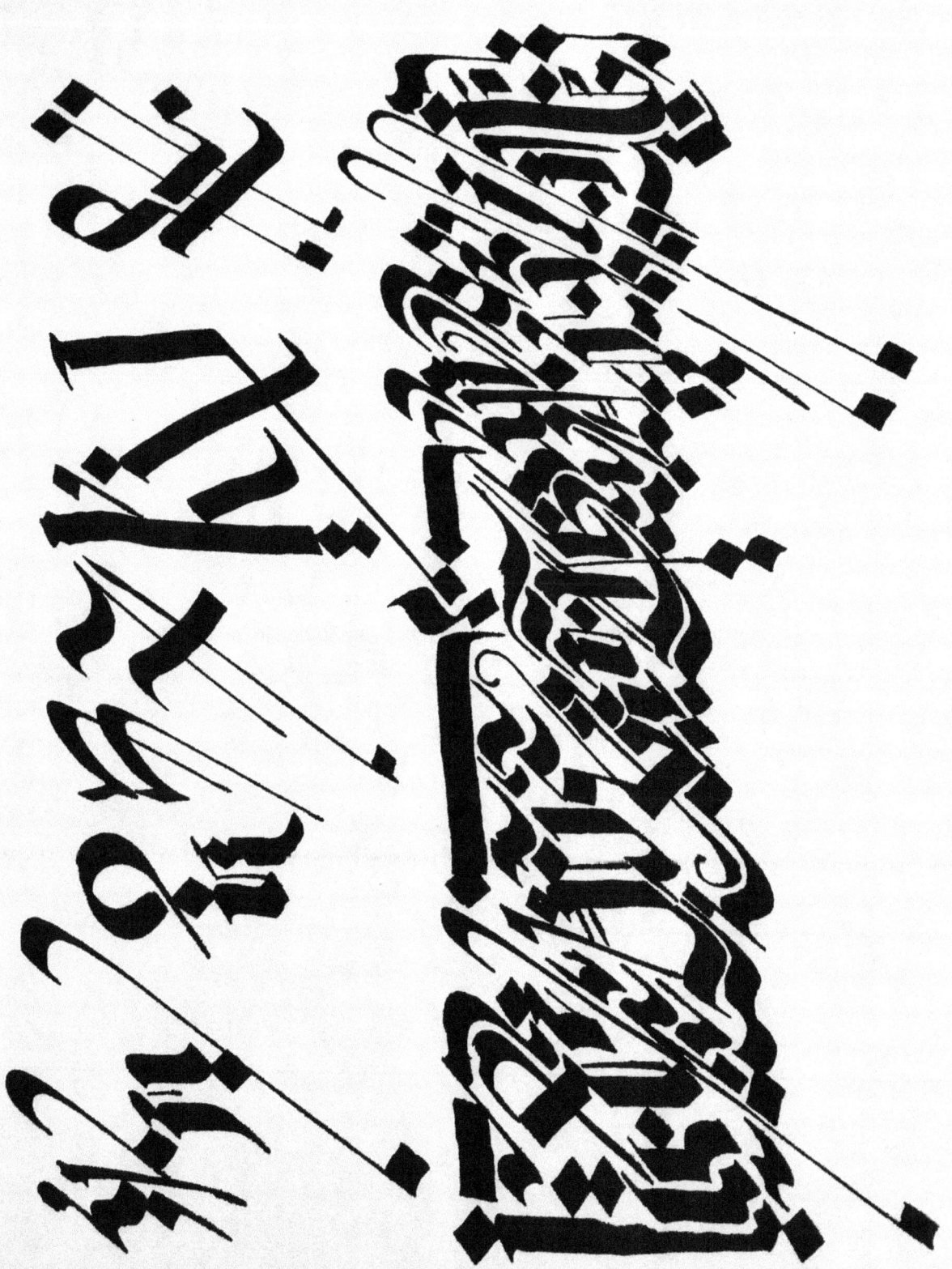

Time Bind

gloomrose, mourners ground to polish, smoothed in the tumbler
by words of remembrance

a radiological sound
deepens the timbre of your bones

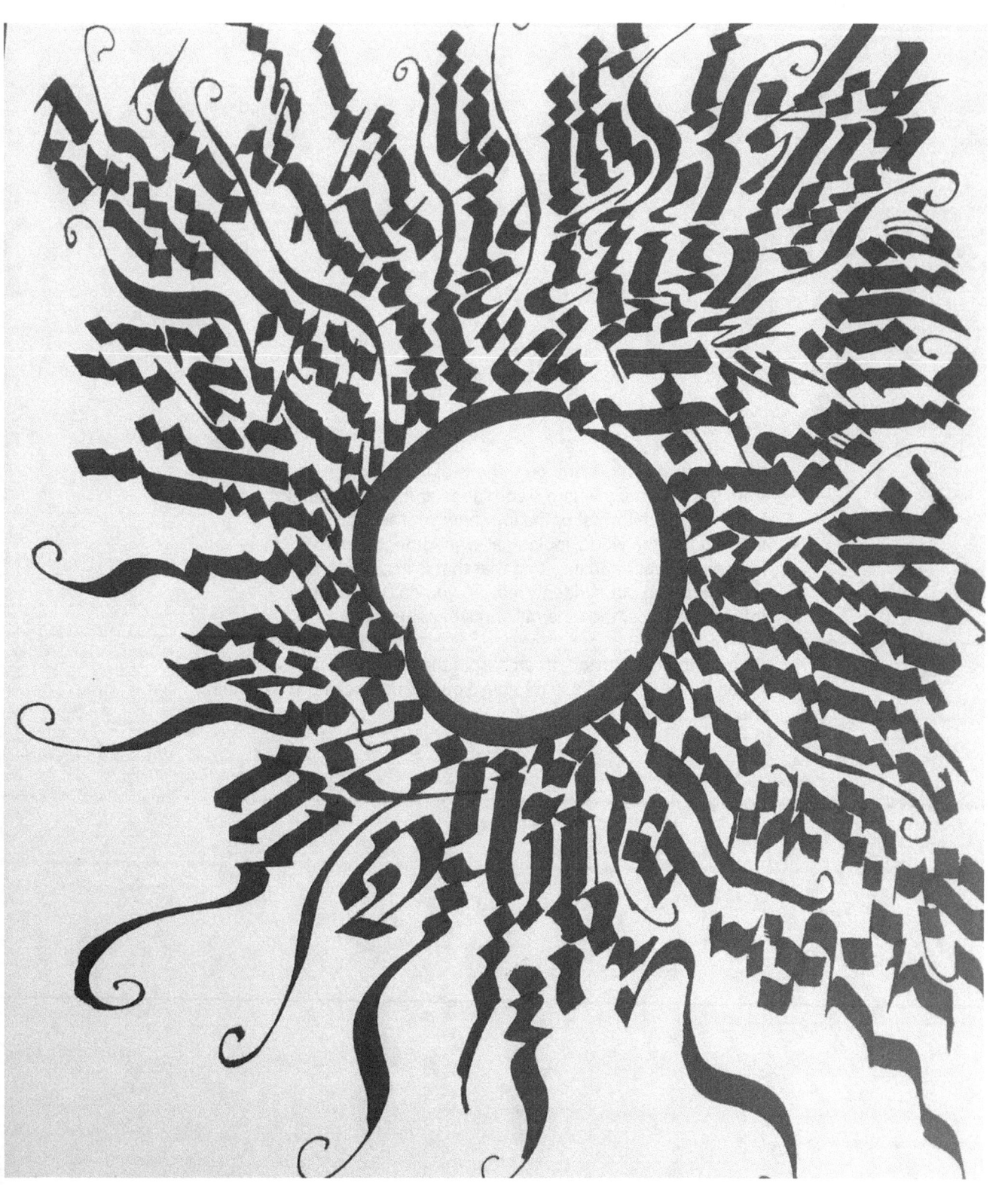

It's critical to think, in the brightness of it, the light
from the pharmacy where razorblades and blood results
lurk among the lowest of the low, how your behavior
is a reflex to the world, looking at what other children
are crying about and insisting that that is important too,
the light going out suddenly leaving you dazzled by its
intense absence, then the millennia of adjustment.

So purchase the cotton dreams, spin the fabric to a dress,
moon-white, you can use it to buy your name back from the witch,
then inscribe it in stone.

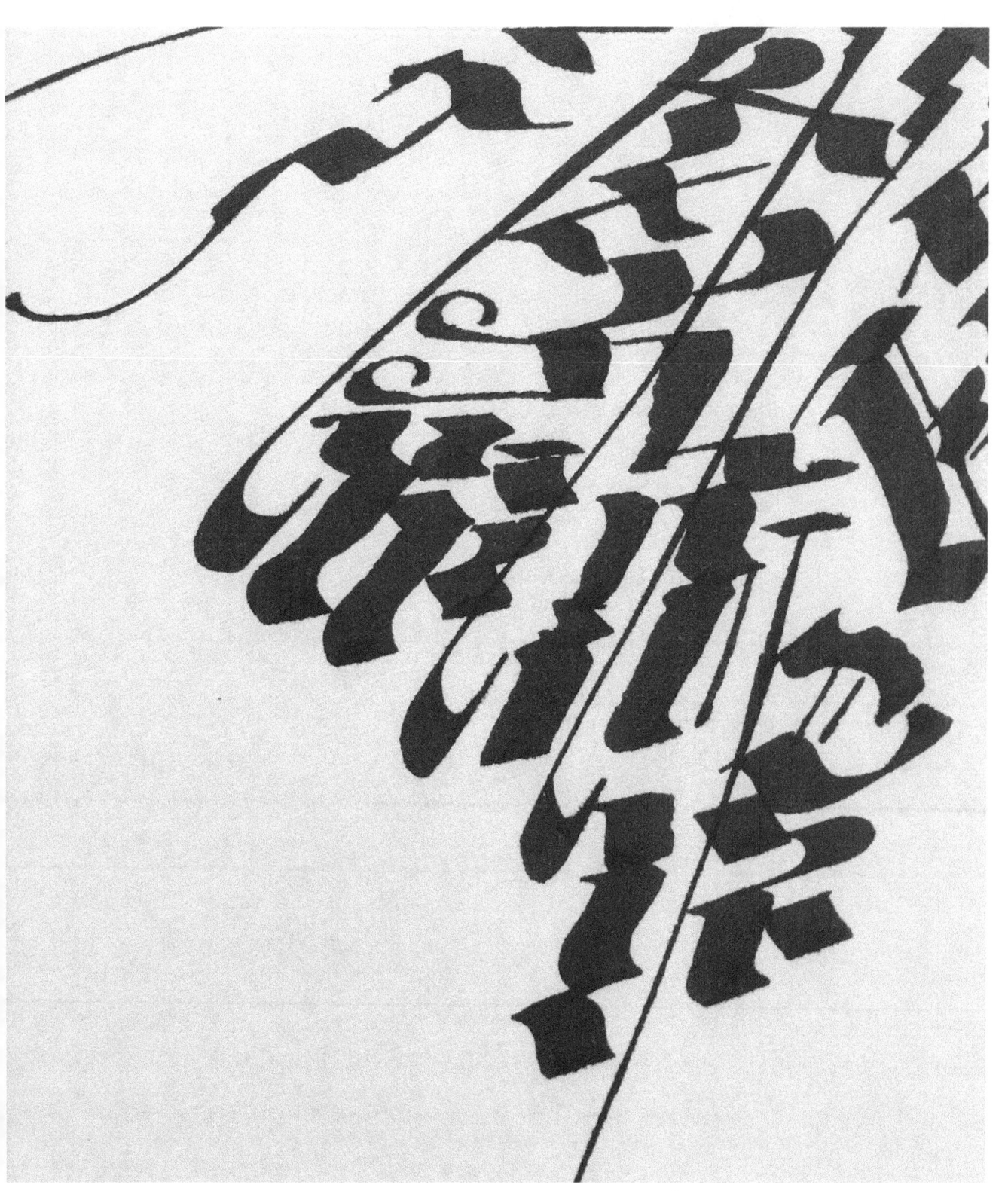

The word for house is pale,
                          drooping
                    from your lips like a drying flower,

so low the earth touches it like a fingers to your breast,
                                          naked and bleeding.

Learn that you were destined for smoke
                          and confusion,

                    for the bright combustion of despair

as you stumble through the barrier bushes,
bringing your groceries home.

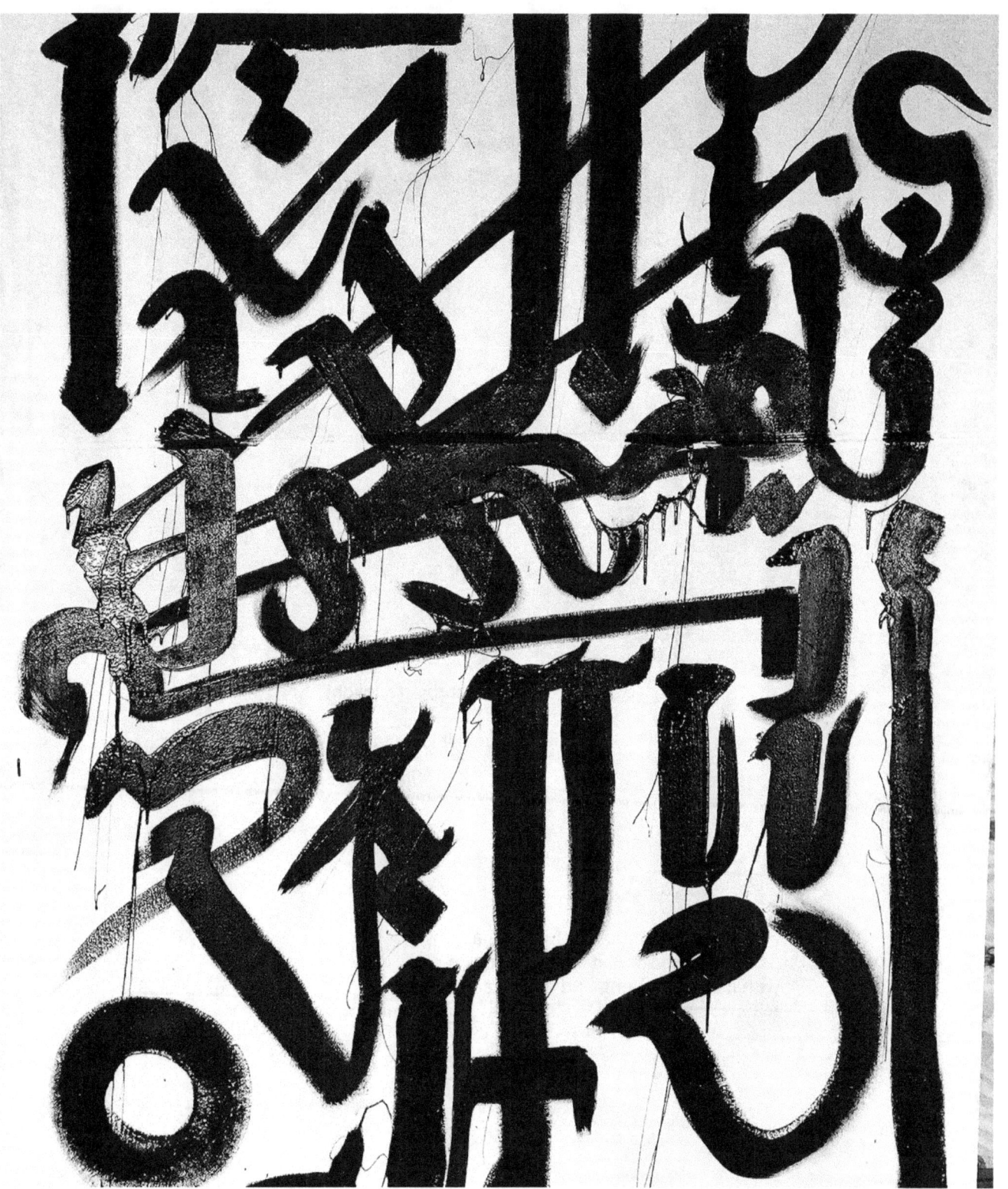

Burnt field, hush as dogs
                    numbered
                            in a ledger,

            waiting.

        Dark also, the dogs
                    like fields of cinder,

        charcoal absorbing sunlight

                until it is mute.

Held back from moonlight, there's a blow
as though the street itself had struck me
with its black torrent, and it feels a blasphemy
to be so poor in spirit, so unable to hear the ringing.

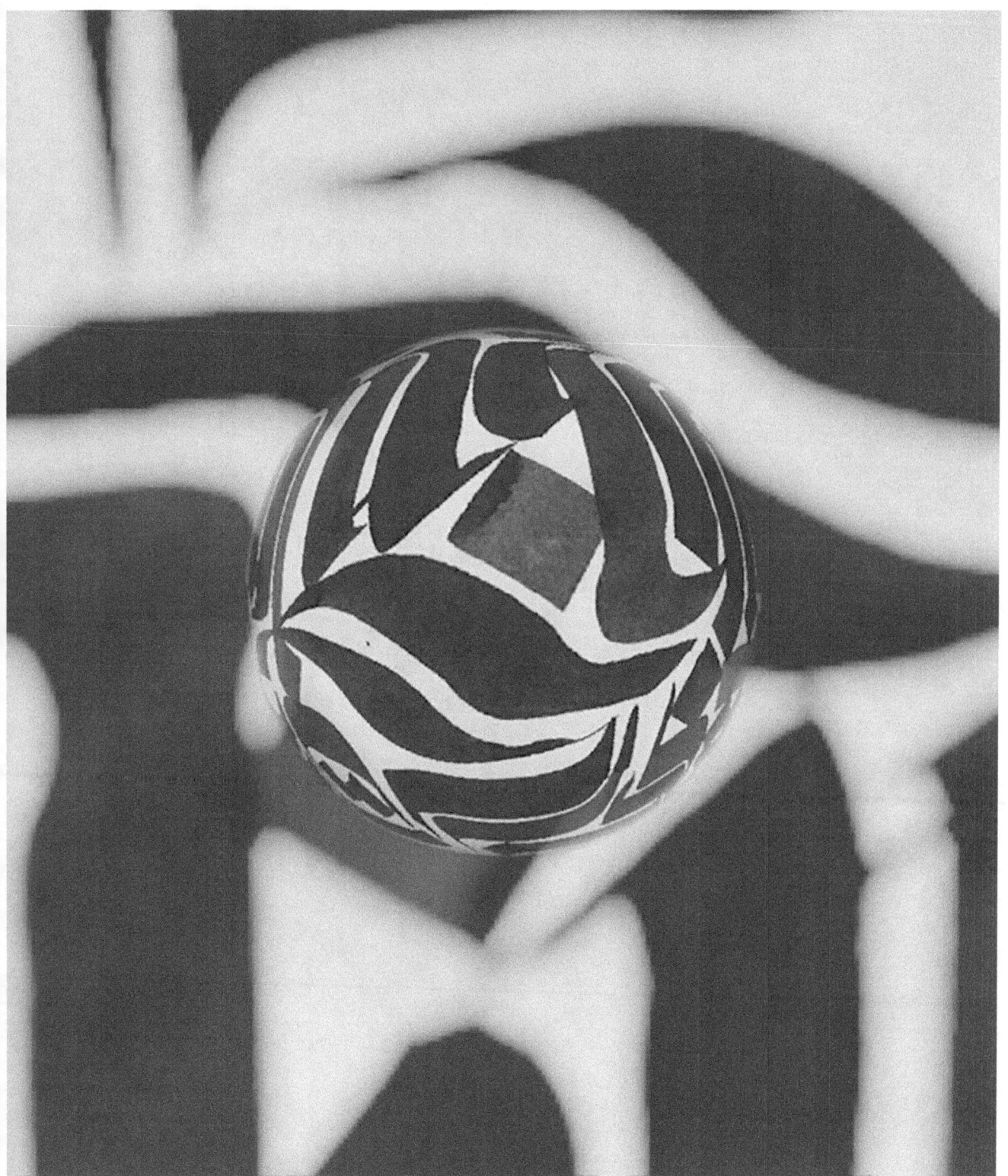

The mortuary branch --

where you hazard to be chaste, the sybil indexes

a passage of seasons themselves, the stones live light, each hollow

a recollection.

I surrender my human resemblance
                        and set free
                        the thousands of shadows
                        I rendered, set them free

                        like smoke rings
                                to rise and linger
                                and diffuse

                                to be breathed
                                by you,

                                beautiful
                                        absorber,

                        terrible beginning.

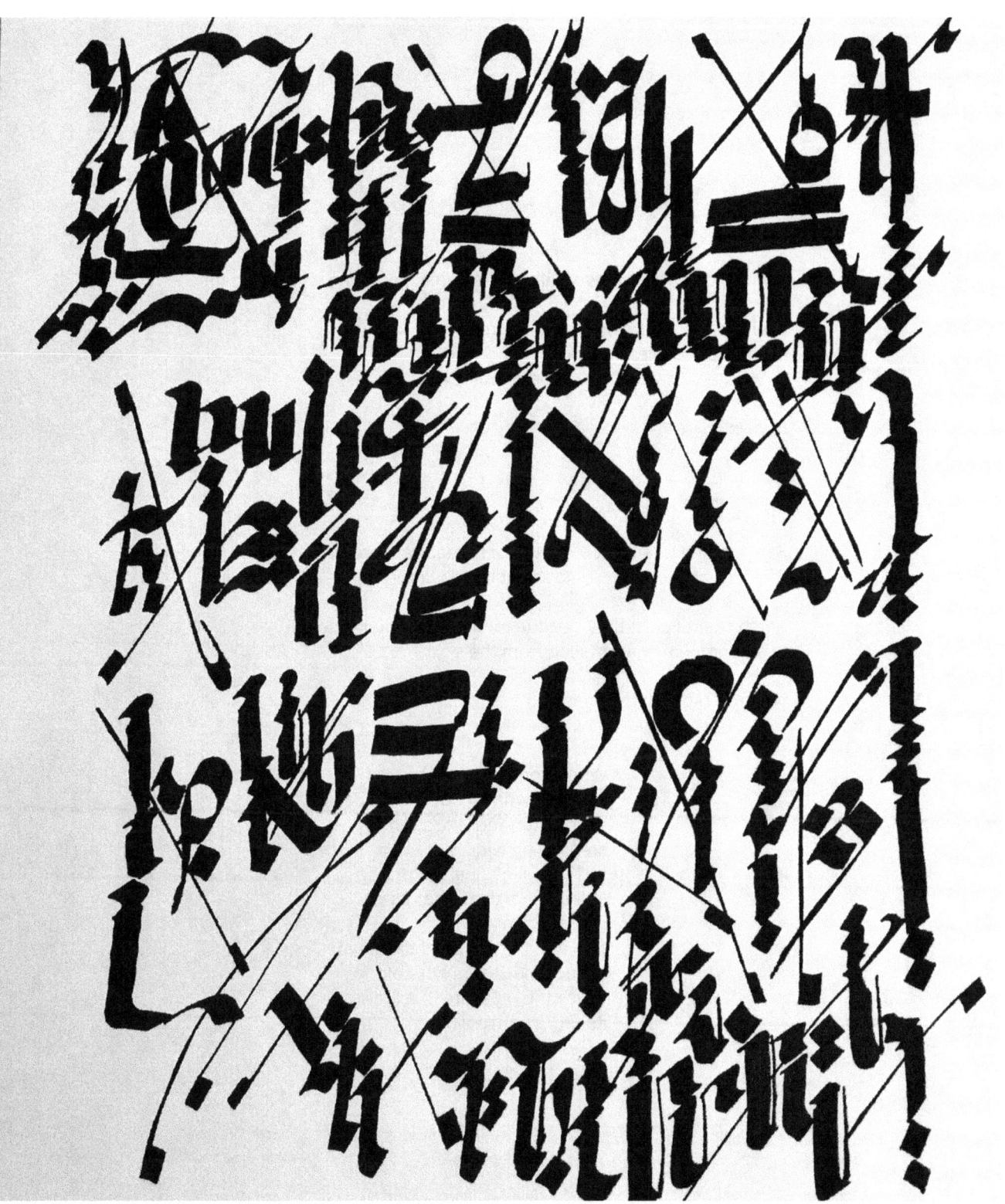

I was told to go and hide; that in the game, someone would find me.

And I went into the arms of pine tree,
its litter of needles
                            a premonition

to pain.

I hid and no one has yet to discover
my absence.

Salvaged children, ink blotting the notes, water-run blue
                            to the color of winter sky,

harsh sky reflects, they say, the memory of water, science
in a handful of stones fallen from the sky.

Nature's modern mesmerisms

                    What stones I have stacked
                    to order, what shadows they cast
                    over water; the lake's remove
                    creased by wind also, also
                    the casual glance, disturbing
                    in the wind, the flutter I saw
                    you give me
                                trembled the trees
                    naked also, it was not cold,
                    it was the measure of a stone,
                    its arc, its shadow.

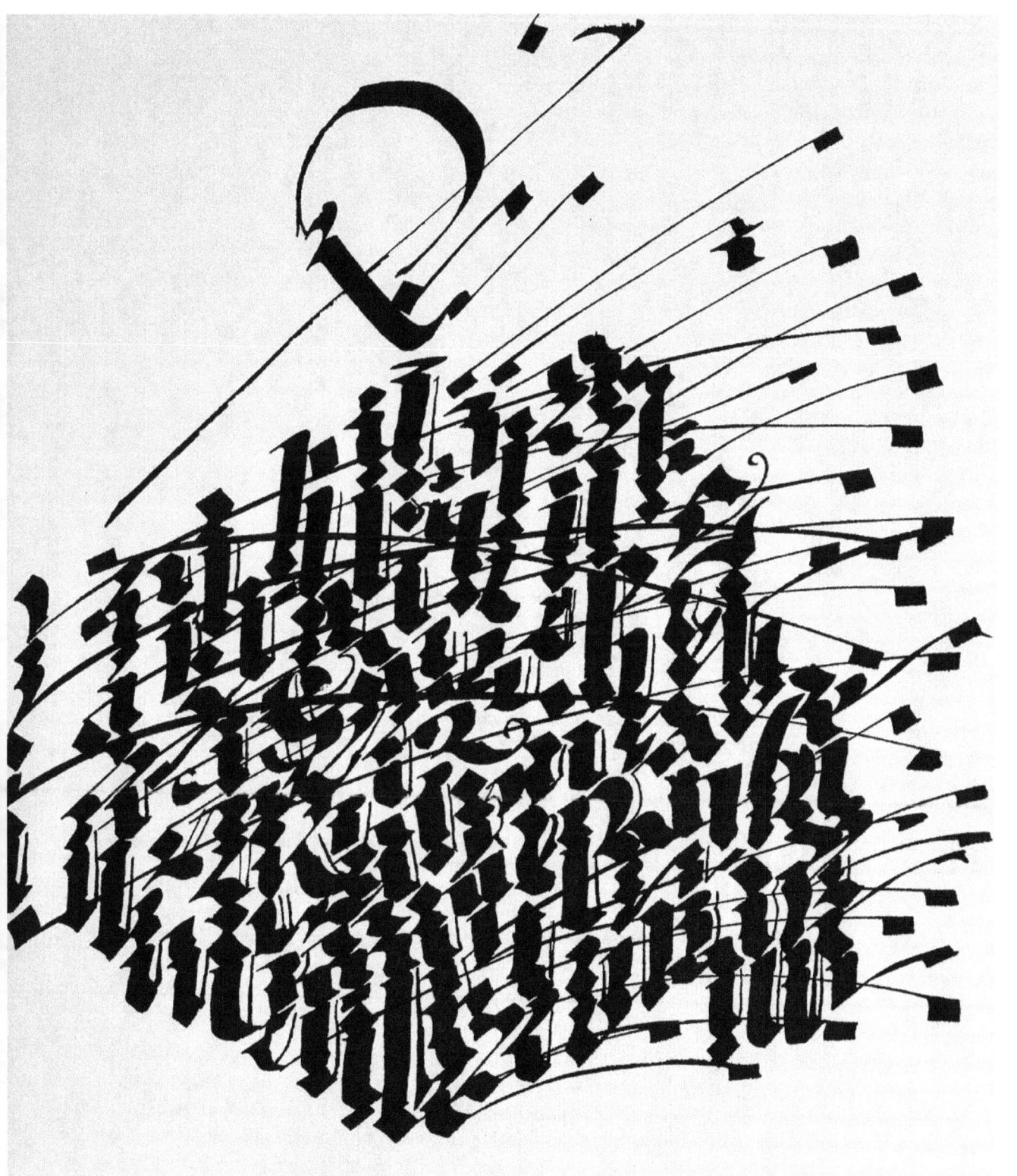

Mix the ash into your bread flour
with a knife of dried blood,

rite of presage -- the shut up heart.

Dogs speak over and over
the same word,
                speak to the comet

just as the stones are laid upon the condemned,

                give thanks
        and count as high as you can.

The virus stirs uneasy in all your white throats, reveals the superstructure like a
bone protruding from a new break,

                new dawn.

                Blood-round like a medallion, made from new
courses of metal, rounding to ornament.
                The glass on the road sheens with applause.

I'm made of these fragments, the sun dying through me, so painful.

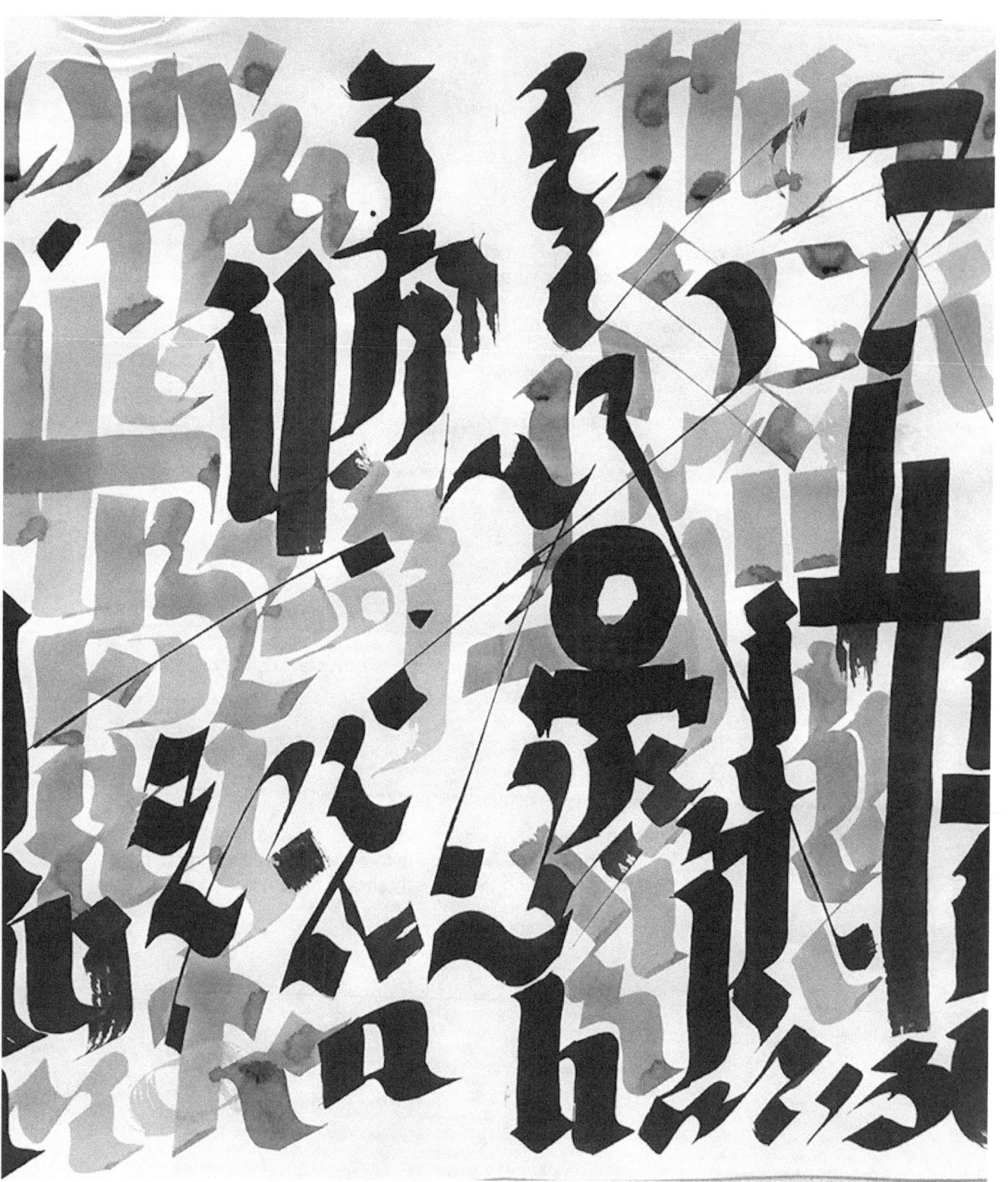

I said, when shall we die? And it might be as it rains.
And it will be a weekday for sure.
                                        But you
will say my name and it will not be me.
                                        I will
still be dead, and it will be ordinary also

to count out the rainfall until it is effigy.

Enough. Over your skin it is cool and poisoned.

The search party flashlight beams split poplars, cover leaf damp, bobbing
sickles of damp.
My beam is fading.
                Anemic,
                I am draining
                myself

of childhood trauma.
                        The outside rings on the tree stump are corroding to paper,
to poem, to prepositions, calling to the lonely shovel, here, here.

Your phone is ringing, leaking out the night.

Look down at your hand, something,
                                a souvenir coin,
                                pressed and elongated

as though at an amusement park
but bearing my name,

                        novelty with no currency.

The golden spur prods you until you answer

the message on the temple frieze,
                                angel abandoned pediments

become delinquent and dropping stones on the heads of travelers, who turn their
faces up to get a stone in the eye; eyes down, a ping in the fontanel,

the soft panel of brain mended over with the sickly cast of pale angel's feet.

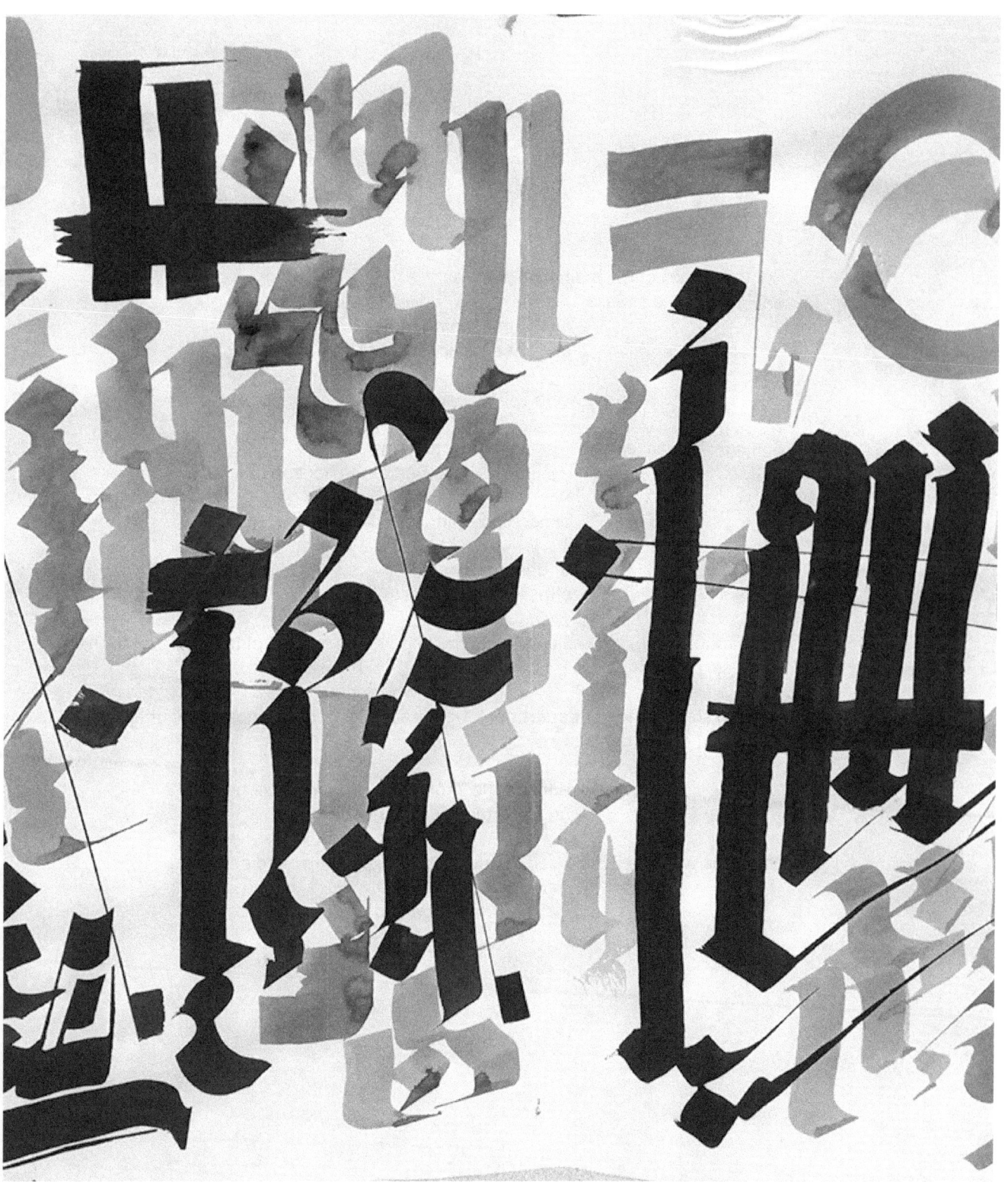

Put the stones of my brain in a glass jar
until they make a plaza,

                    one with echoing foot falls
                    and sheer obscenities of light.

      All the world will be edible.

See how the glass bends the light, its intention.
                            Bends the horizon to a bird's wing,

                    pinion shredding into destiny

                    or derangement,
                    either way, spiritual,

like a rough cloth and walking the entire pilgrimage, instead of taking a taxi, to the
lord's sacrifice.

Uneven steps up to your apartment, train tracks littered with goats. Beautiful
aristocrat, god of denial,

                    denude the virgin's statue with a ball-peen
                    and a fortune-teller's needle.

Inject me with the wind. Use a murky fluid and a gliding needle,
                    murk and blood-cloud,
                            the beggar's divestment.

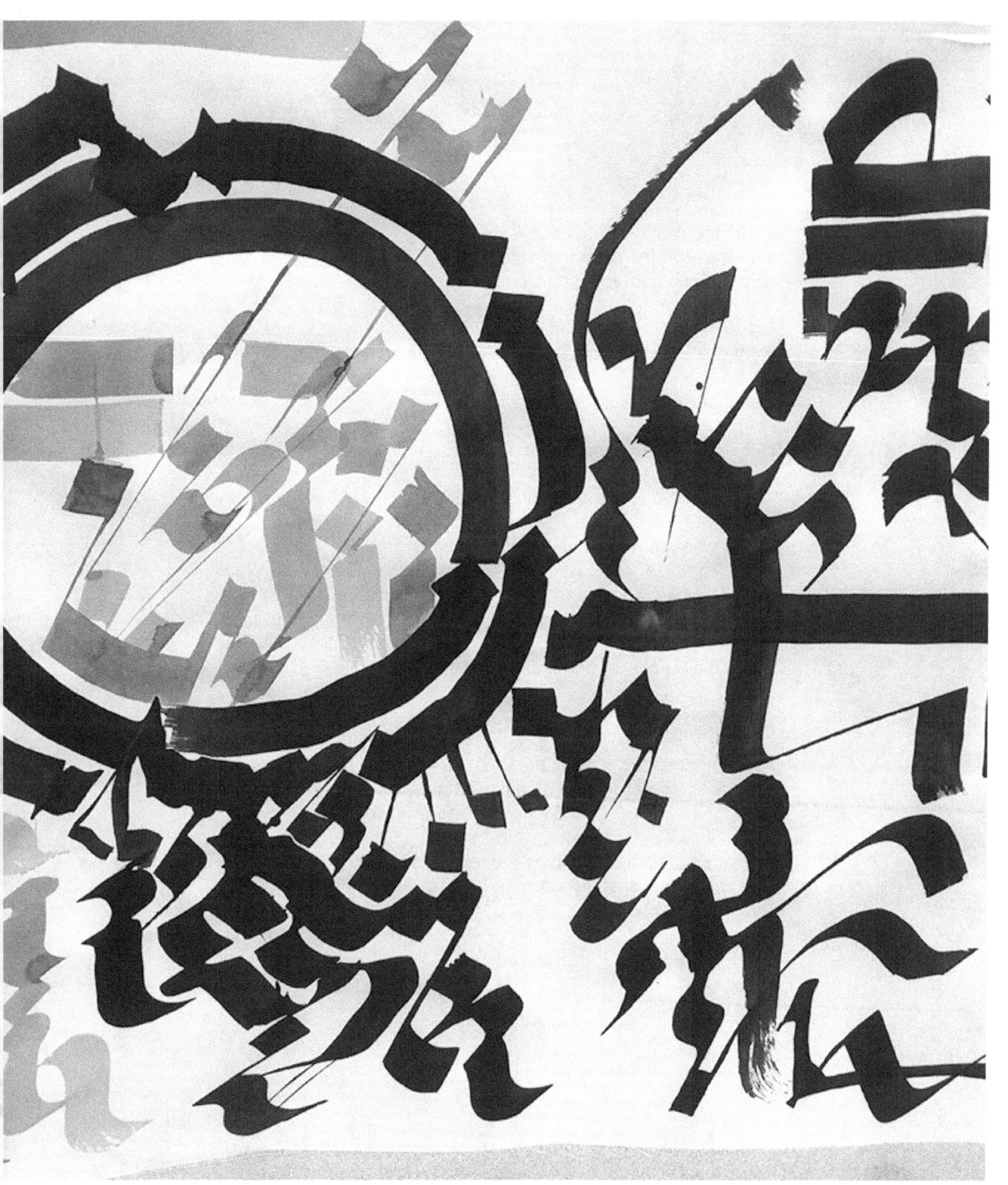

Fill up the past with stones. Fill your mouth
with the past, the gleaming, rotten past,
volumes of blood-vomiting stone,

fissure mouths scraped off of statues,
centuries on relief scraped by the guillotine of eyelashes,

clamp down on everything on fire.

Here is a word to spread limit upon,

                         the infinite, limit
                                     upon
so you don't turn to stone in its face.
                        I am shouting
                        at you until even the air
                                    is solid.

Learn the lexicon of mannequin's tongue,
                        my little box of blood
                        is staggeringly French.

I can't understand a word, but then I never could penetrate your twilit aura, the
shadows rising around to myriad windows,
                      fenster ad fenestrum seculorum.

Coin my slot with bobby pins, I'm ready, I say with an offhand hip, an armlessness
that speaks of constellations.

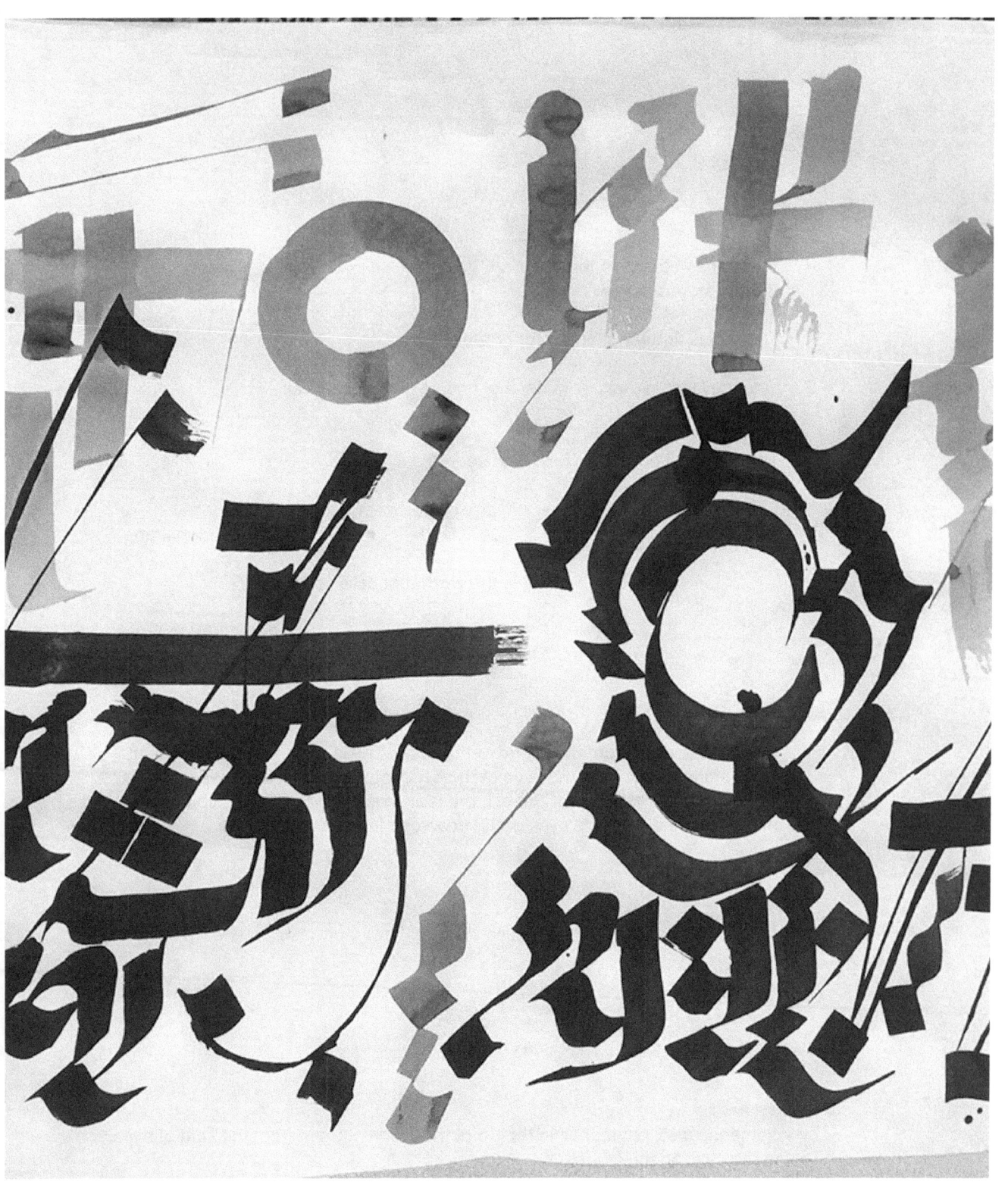

The stones belong to the dead.
Put the stones in your mouth.

The leaves fluttering, grope for ground.

One grey leaf sounds its stiffening, finds a grip in your hair.
I pull it out.

This cross-stitches your face with sound,
                              crumbles
                              and pieces rise again,
                                        vein and tendon lifting.

                 What is the word that calls you to me?

Harvest the dead from the island of the living. The island in the ocean of salt.
If the stones grow from the eyes of the dead into crystal trees, trees of air and
electricity, then we can eat them. If the island of salt makes it possible to arise out
of the expanse, then the eyes of the dead can feed us with stones.

If someone dies, put stones in their mouths. Harvest them from the field of eyes.
Put the eyes on the stones.

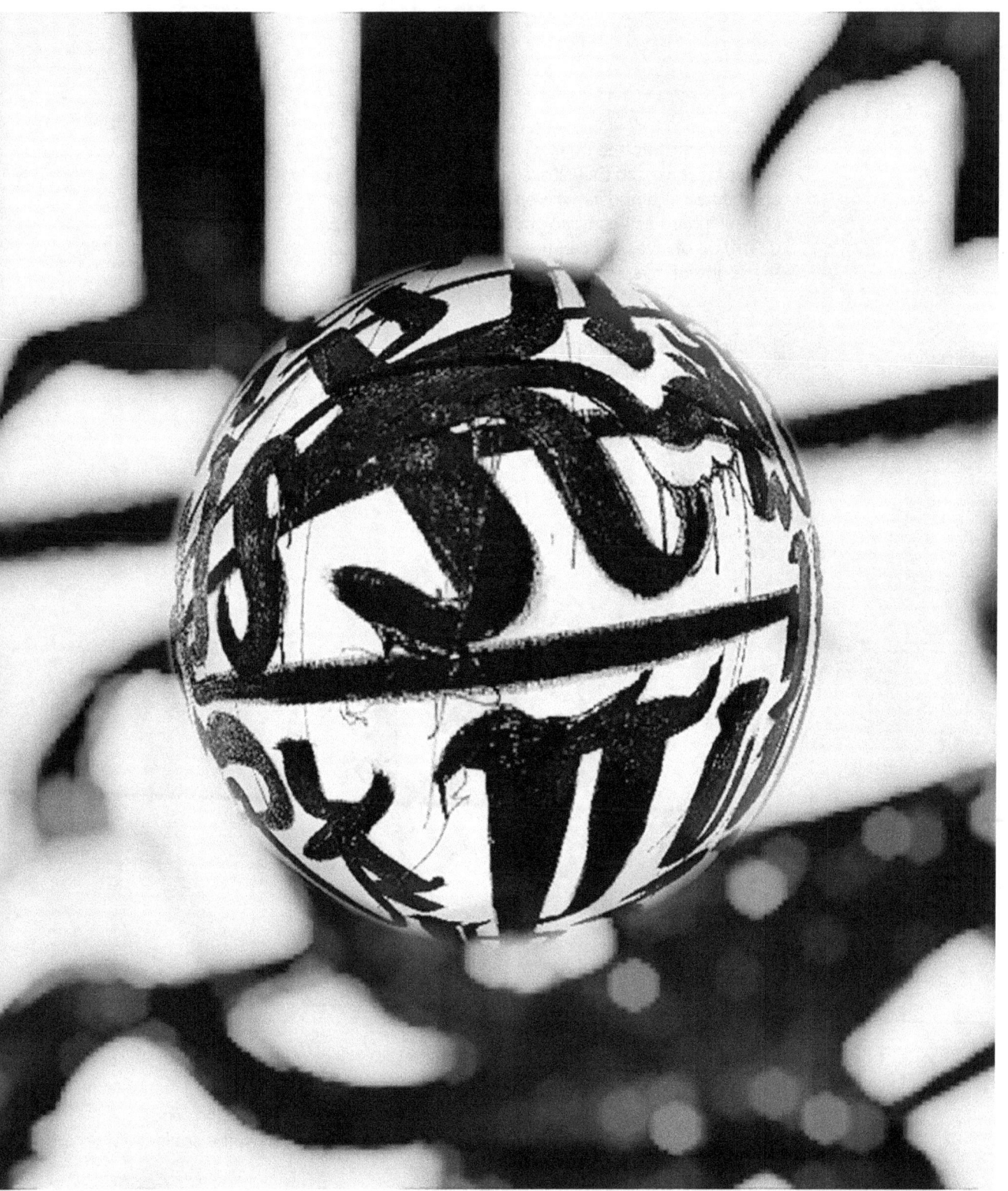

I throw rocks into the quarry water
as hard as I can, so they strike your towns
and homes and ghosts who speak the harrowed fields,
I throw it hard as I can into your heart, into the deep
quarry pit of love, so I can hear its obligations echo,
the sound of myself among the clouds.

Turn your eyes away from the starvation of the night sky. That expanse will
consume you, you will be pulled into the space of stone.

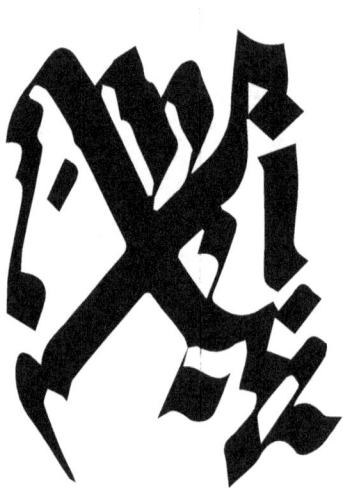

Do not use these rocks to strike tears from another's eyes.
Every stone is a number, and every number equals the name of god. And
every stone carries the weight of space inside it, holding down the souls
to a space in the galaxies of quartz.

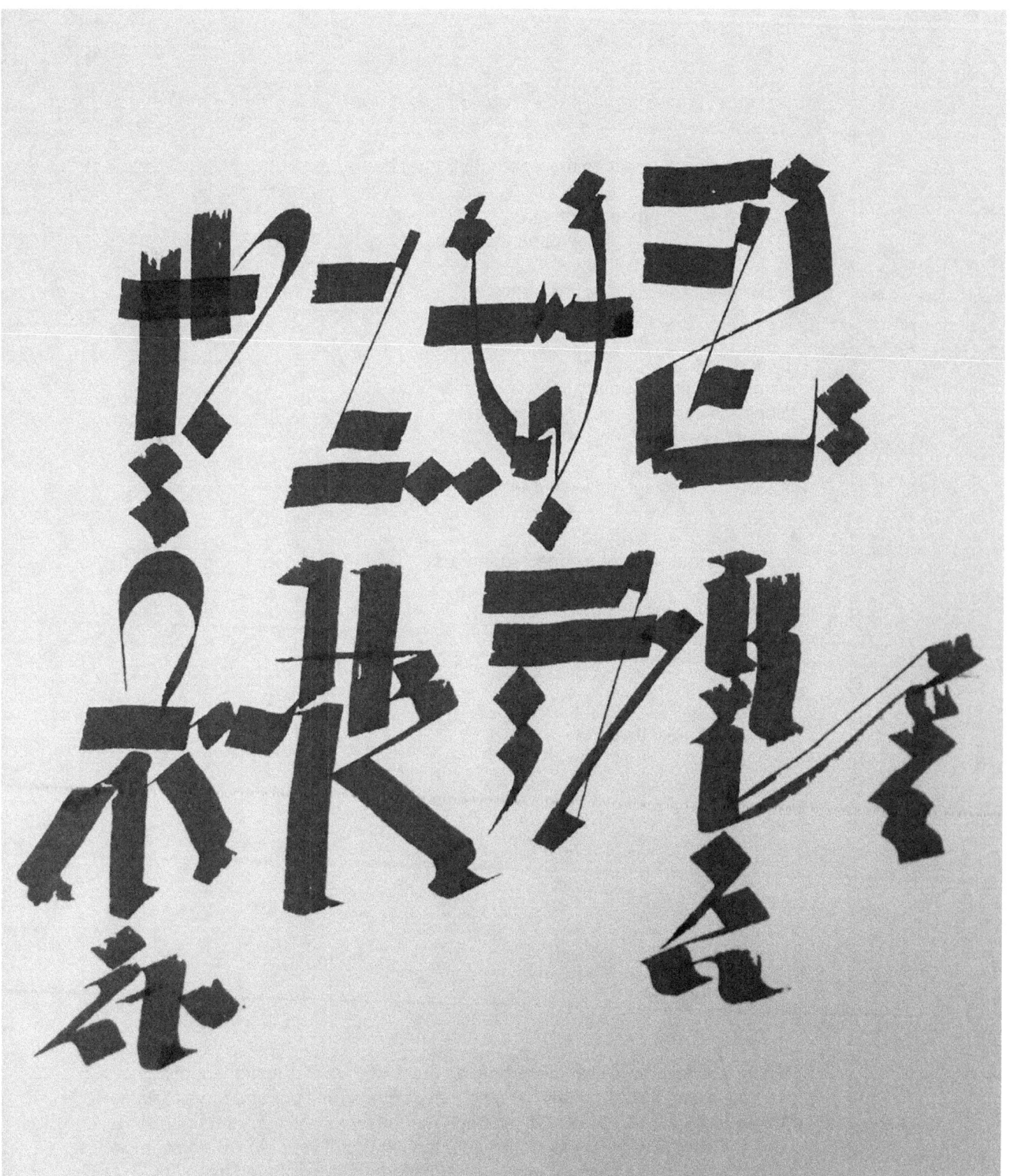

Dear Ancient, I speak to the weathering I will be

       mad to remain
             wet on the page.

         Ink honed
    to stillness.

Dear Ancient,
hammer-split the jagged line of concrete
along the canal, the one, like your heart
edged to perform
resistance.
       Ancient, raise your arm,
           sweetly
      hold up a
    a look of gentle edged segments

but keep the waters down,
keep at bay the tumbling
stones all of your city's houses

Keep yourself from giving in
to the tongue of the river.

There will be a day to set everything on fire. I offer up this testament of stone,
so you may strike it from my hand so that as it hits the floor and turns to flame
it will burn my heart black with shame. And the rivers will burn, set upon stone,
and the streets will burn as stones, and the wheels of your car will flame in circles
of light until they disappear into the dark where there will be no more fire.

The moon is crumbling also, giving up her precious
bonds, stone by stone.

      Sailor's captivated
      by her luster make tiny temples from her tears.

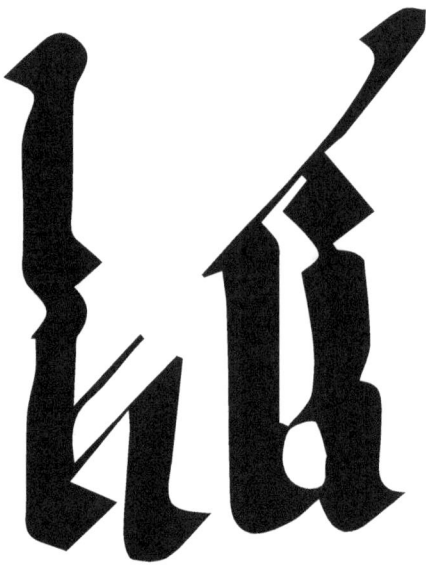

And an unbillowing, like deflated lungs, as when a net bag of fruit is severed from
below, the stones of my eyes will sour until they gleam and forget.

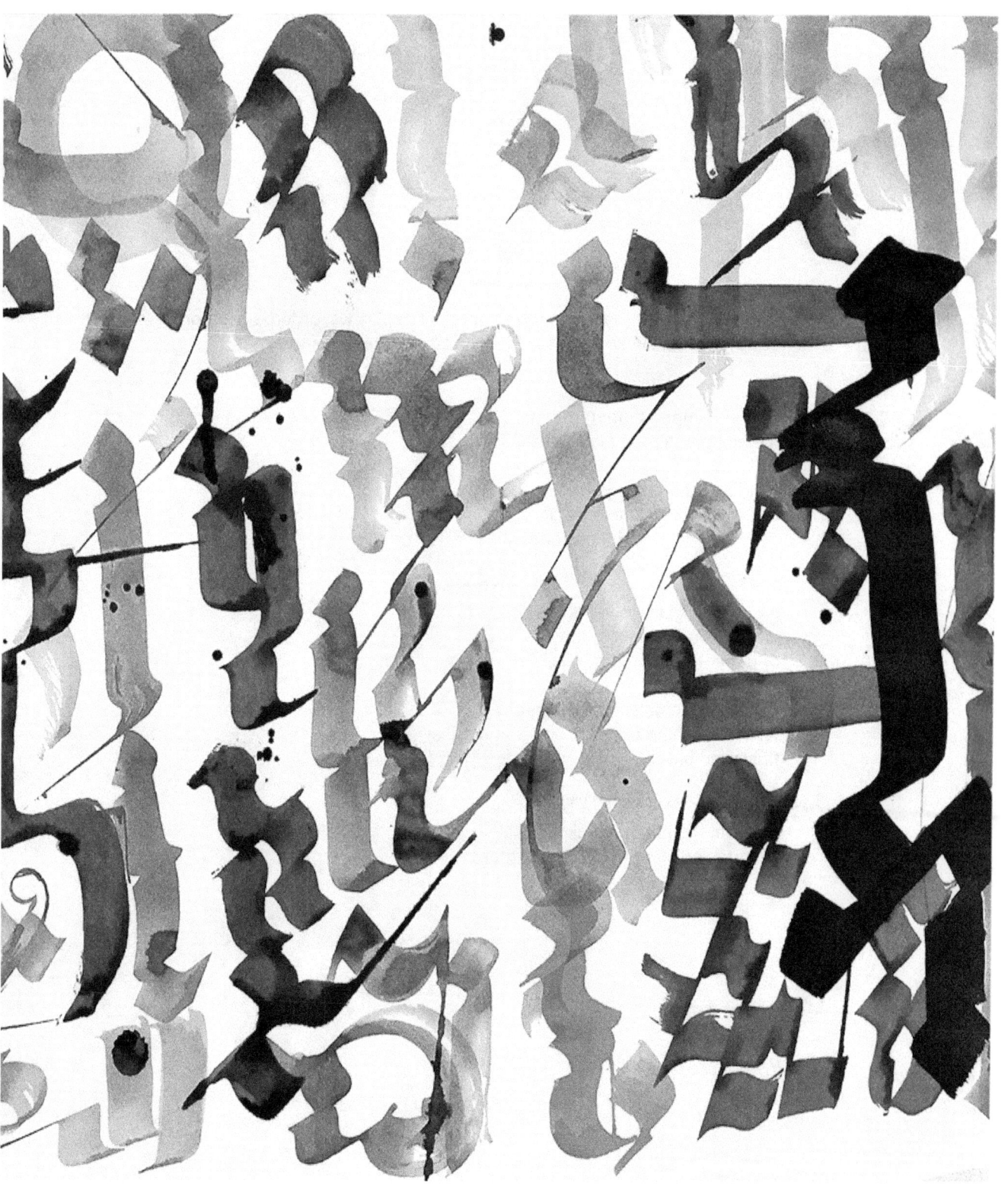

The specimens in boxes, rest on cotton, in neat rows, ordered like horses passing at a steady gait. Fixed but adrift, like a comet's wake of the past.

Like a diamond planet
the stone of a pear elongates in glass,

a brilliant thing in a jar
              crescent bent,
              princess finger,

                            slender
blued with glaziers veins
       and careful folds
of paper like cut diamonds,

the stone trembles in the glass
where touching fingers bend and crease,
flush and bare,

neither bird nor vase or boutonniere
can fold the fingers back
to touch again what once was there.

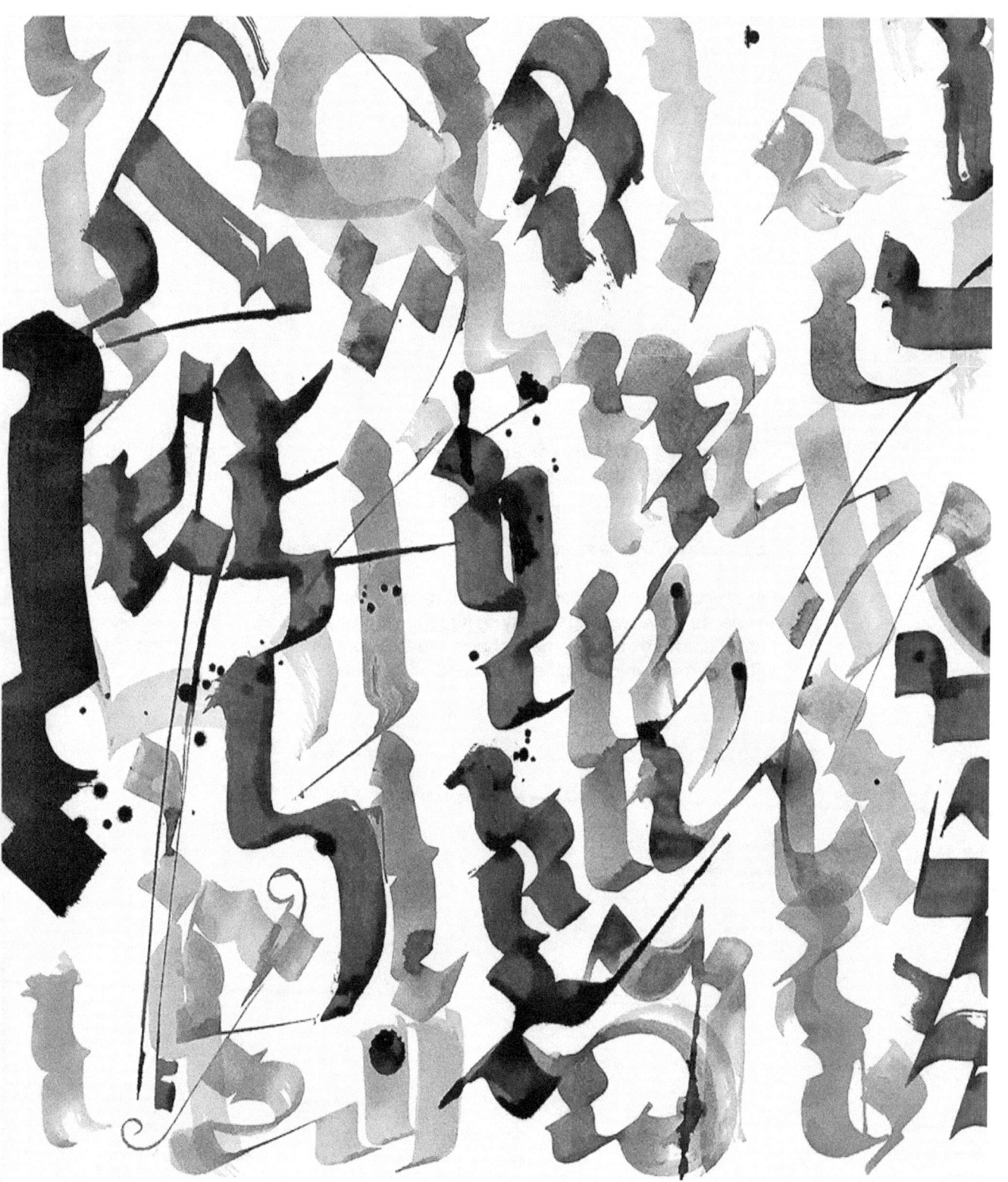

Carbon dating finds a ring of faces around a fire, a ring of black stone prodded by a stick. The white coals at the bottom will remember. There are fifteen little stones in my shoe, reminders of the generations I walk upon.

Past aura, smile on a spike, I watch you hold as you speak.

Oh country, now you sleep, encased in mirrors. I look in
the pecan grove, tearing the sky so it founders, penumbra
sunset aperture on my camera phone, the trees are laden
with sparrows which erupt at the sound of sky's fall.

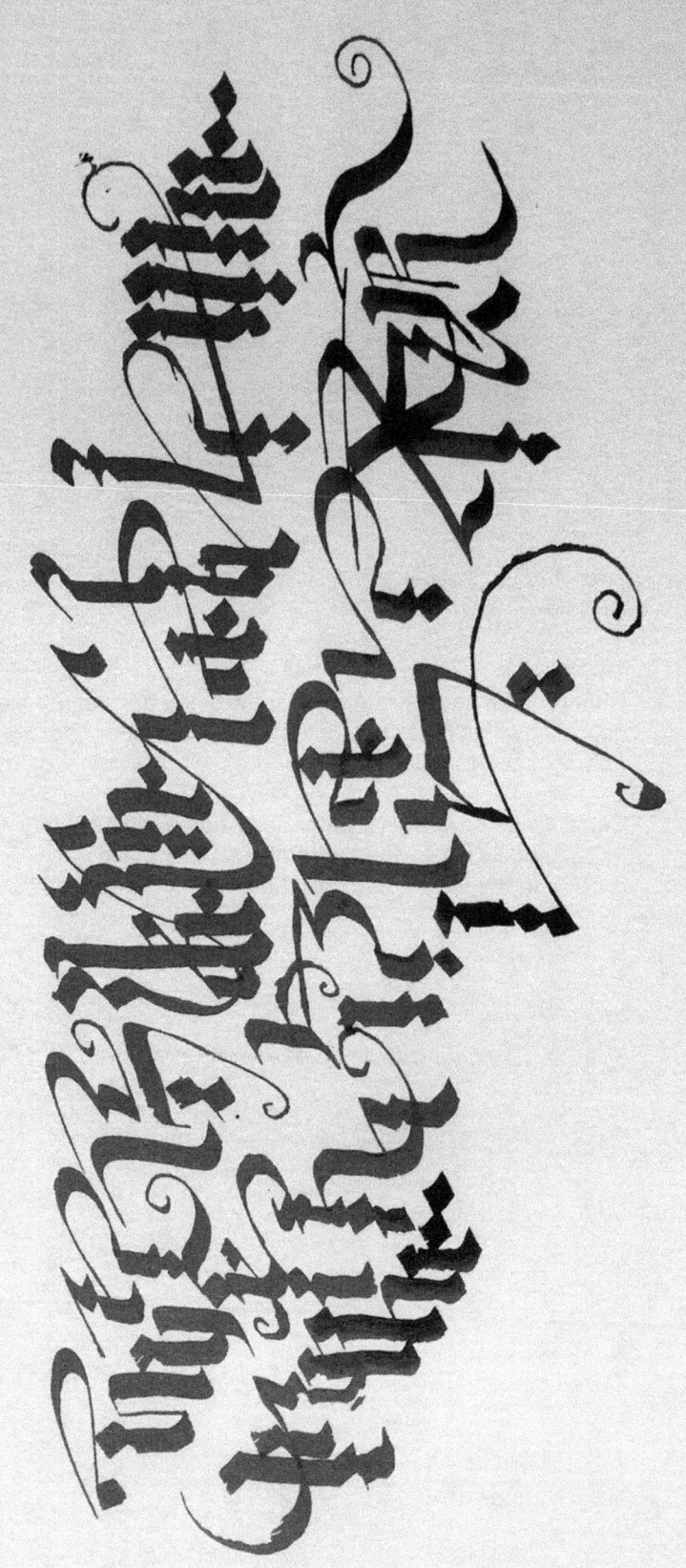

I'm mixing up some grout to clear away the gaps in the tile. The clean floor will not rot. It will tell the story of standing, the feet of god, his fortress. The pattern of righteous tears, a tiled memory.

Cups of silence, useless, water dripping on the mortality
        of my cards, the future of cups marshalled
        in the bartenders row. Piercing southern heat.

I can't remember you.
I threw a stone at you.
It was my name,
it had a dream in it.
It was an egg,
it wouldn't crack.

I was open but there was nothing coming out.
I opened myself expecting blood,
but nothing came out.
I was empty,
so I filled myself with stones,
but even they disappeared.

When I found a stone on the road
I picked it up,
I was excited and wanted to share.

I threw it at you to share
my inside. It hit you
and everything was spilled.

Logtruck fills a highway arc, tread to tread
      the rumble irks pecan and pine, trash tree
      and crop, the living blue night.

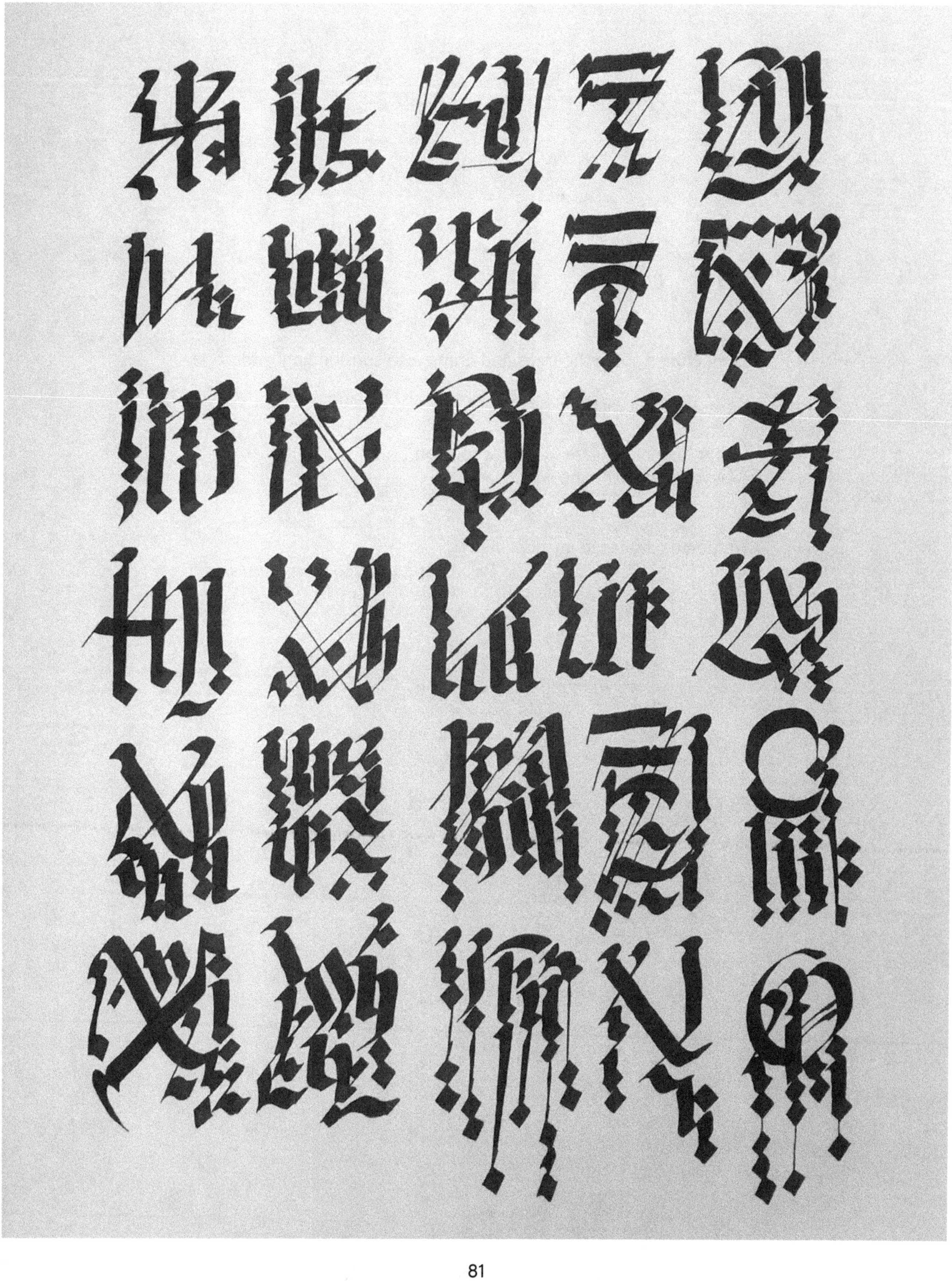

Light comes out of the trees and drafts up a surrounding landscape,

trees, lots of leaves and dirt.

I want to think you are formed whole too,
that you come with the light
                            and not from it.

I'm putting stones in my pockets
                            so I won't drift away to where souls go.

I'm from the cave,
                a smudged figure, poorly
                        blent,
                        coal soot and exhaust,

                    I'm more perfect

                        at failure

than night's abrupt silence.

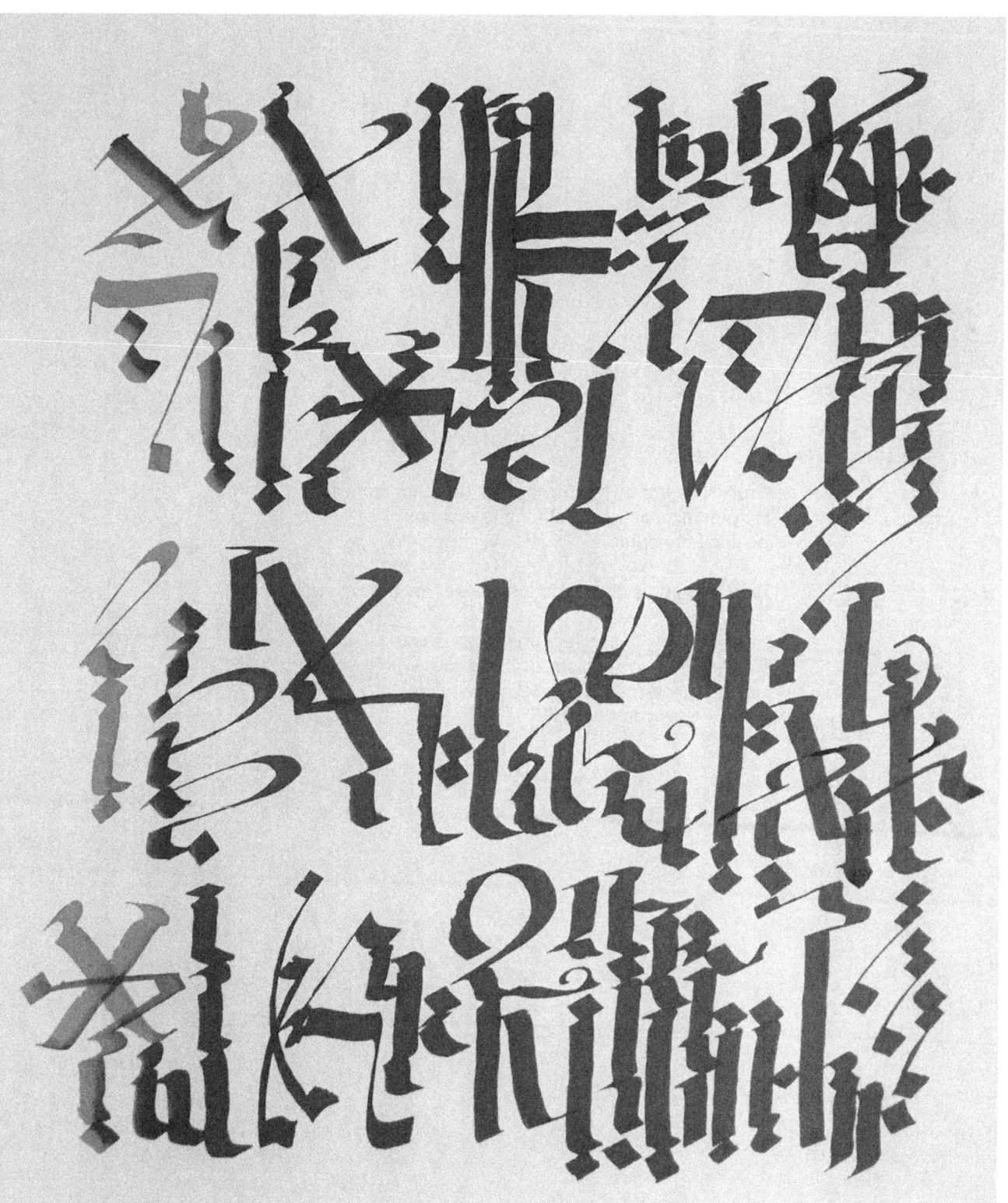

A rockslide from a hillside is like a disco for stones.
They stumble around, bobbing to the music,
looking for a drink.

Then they settle down and look disapprovingly at strangers.

Lines can only fail, valleys and foreheads
both lie down with prayer, both dissolve with touch.
Listen, you can't expect a definition when
        lines can only fail.

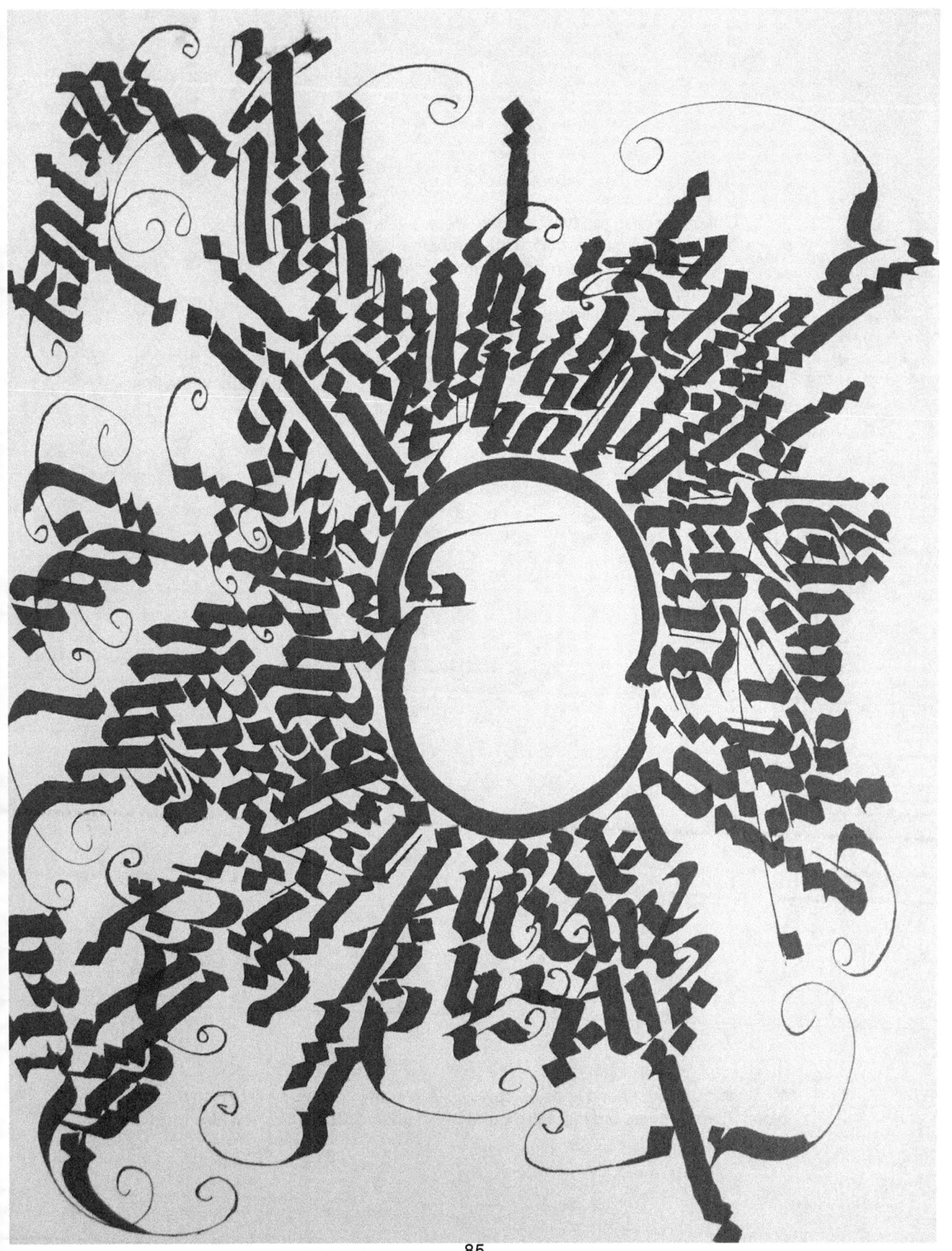

Out of the mist, the twisting bare trees
are dark like women, dark with tremors
and veins against the rubbing light's emergent
rhythm,
          daggered light,
                    and somewhere in the umber
                         an invasive flower, a foreign face, blesses the cold
                                             with clear white lips

Magicians draw deer and lions on cave walls to show warriors how to lose the fear of blood. To show there are more profound things than doors, which will also be invented by magicians.

I've been living in a cardboard box with a tiny window.
It has an array of children's toys, dolls, mostly,
plastic bodies, legs twisted round backwards,
cowboys and soldiers and muscled injection
mold and fused fingers and fins of excess plastic
uncut, uncut tissue, bodies bisected and emptied,
only air, the stone is only air between molecules.

I live here, in the vacuum sucked plastic neighborhood
of a box with a hole. I see you, the hole is sealed
with the wax of my eyeballs.

Put out the lamp so that everyone is blind as the oil sand, blind as the mountains
beneath the sea, blind as the heart of the heart of stone. Gaze spiral, weep. You are
staring too long at the spot on my heart, it will show you nothing. Put out the lamp.

I'm issuing passports to my fingers, in and out of the mittens, through a wedding band and into a mouth, a train of rings, a series of surgical moments.

Stamped finger passport, what is the nature of your visit? Pants, what is the visit, submerged, a liquid, a pressure. I'm feeling around in the sand just below the surf, shell, shell, stone.

The tide lifts its face to mine and dips its lips into my face, query approved.

My countenance is stone, time withered, out of season, sea pocked,
the wind makes sand from my stone, everything conspires,

dawn's kiss undulates with the dune.

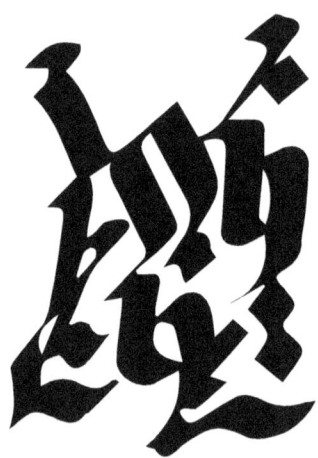

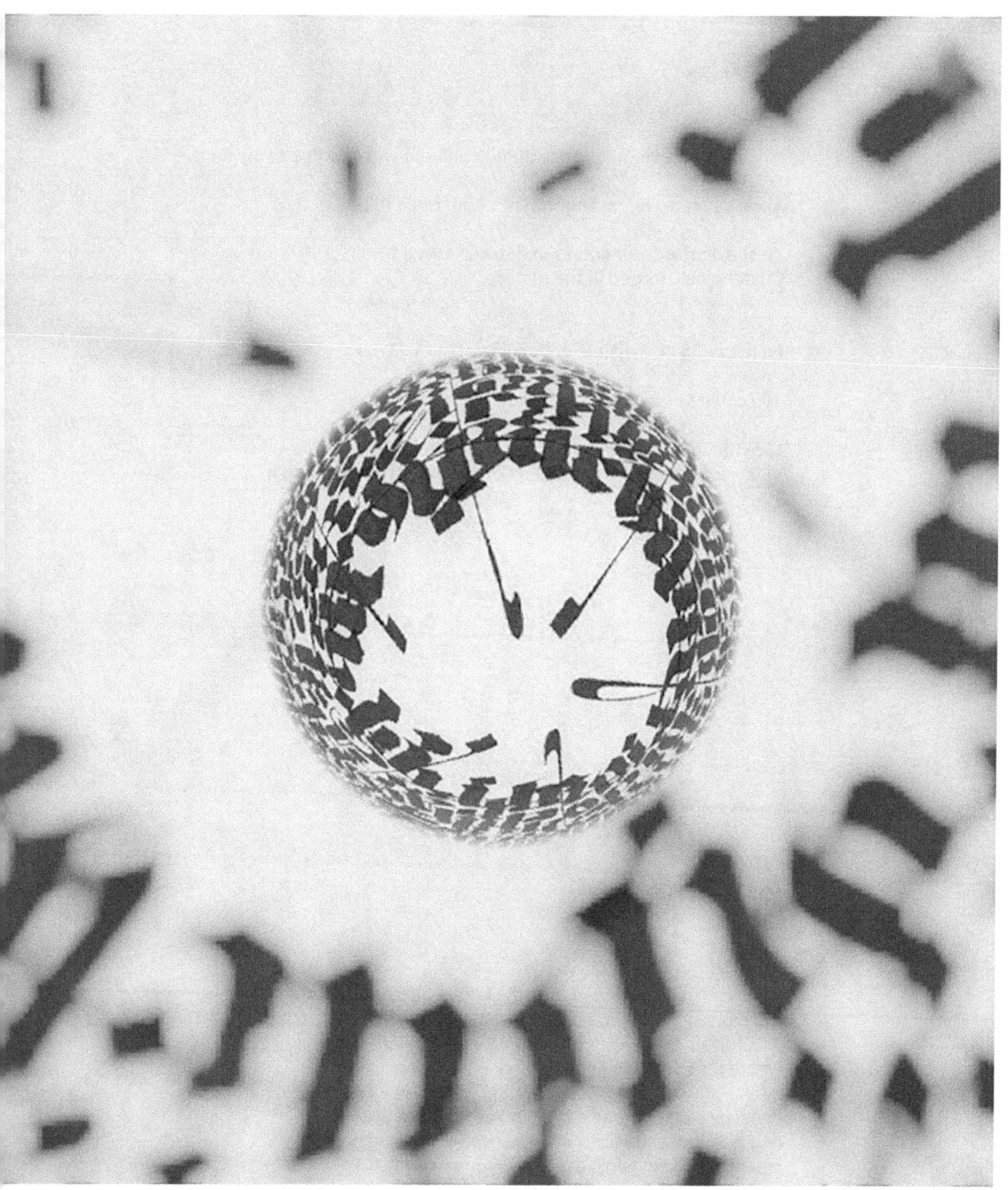

I'm riding a wave of rough textured concrete with the tips of my fingers.

Abrasion, remove my finger prints, I am not a thief.

I feel a dimpled wilderness in the well-formed wall.
Cinder block, forged in the furnace,
                                        we are the same.

I am leaving an invisible dotted line of my skin cells.

You could see it with a black light, splatter sign.

I am trying to reach all the way around the wall
of my school, prison, the footers of my crawlspace, to hold it.

It's a dry road, quiet, and over the land a buzzard lingers
like a prayer to the immense.
                            Wind and the dark spot
where the road dips and demands its toll of oil.
                                            Dry road
beset by stones, stones that flirt with tire damage
and flick their cigarettes into the eyes of passing cars,
cracking windscreens, every so once in a while.

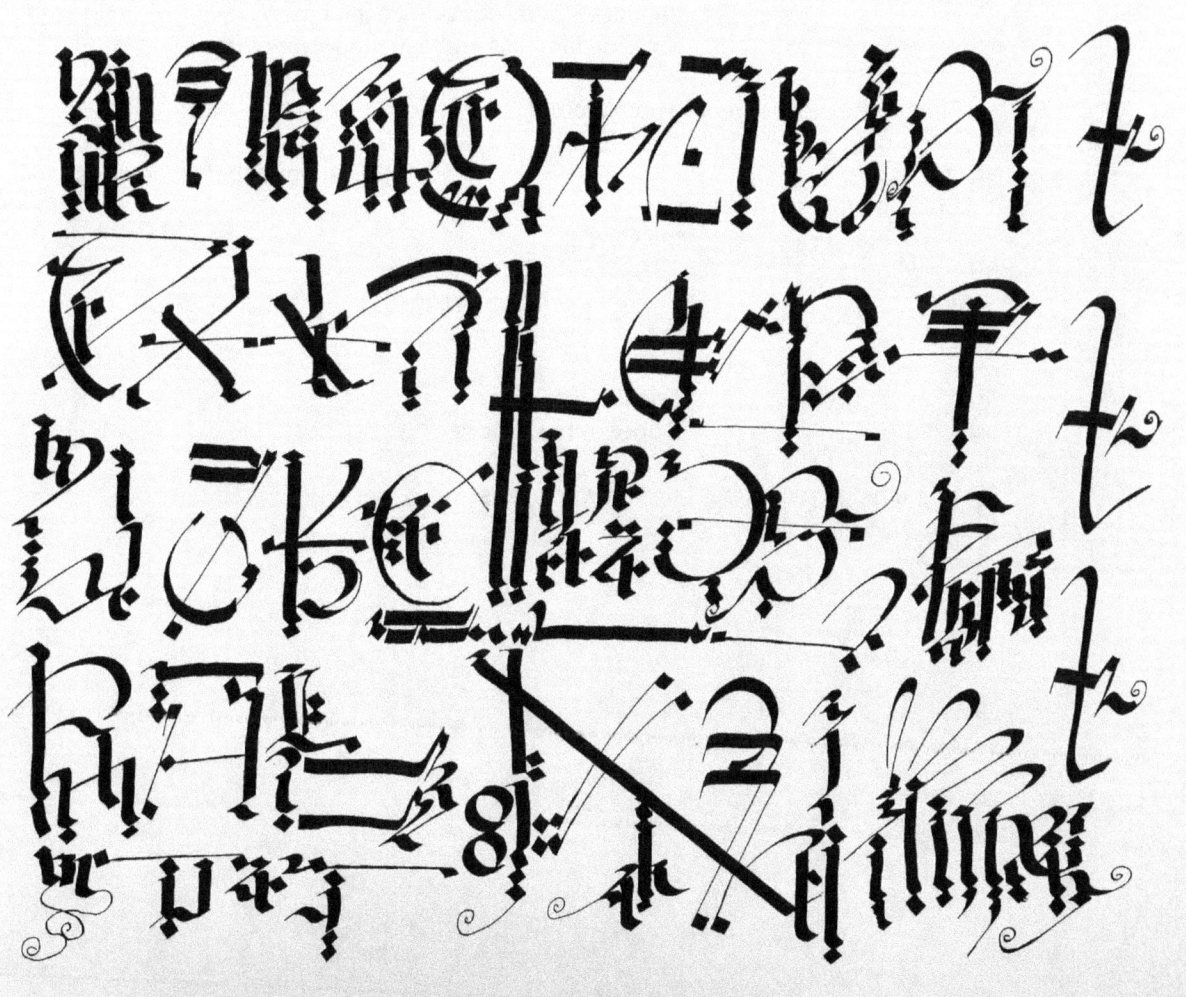

So much detail, so much missing.
                              The capillaries in the eye manage
                    not to interfere in the rummage of my looking,

                    train over there, housing development,
                    some distant hills and a molten river of trees.

Time is the inducement to architecture.

                                        Stones remember smoothness.
But something is missing,
                    the view,
                              your face entering
                              my blood stream
                              through my eyes,

                    calcifies into stone,
                    lodges in my mind.

Something I remember but that won't pass.

Knife in my heart. Harrow the field, knife of terrible stone.
Weeping.

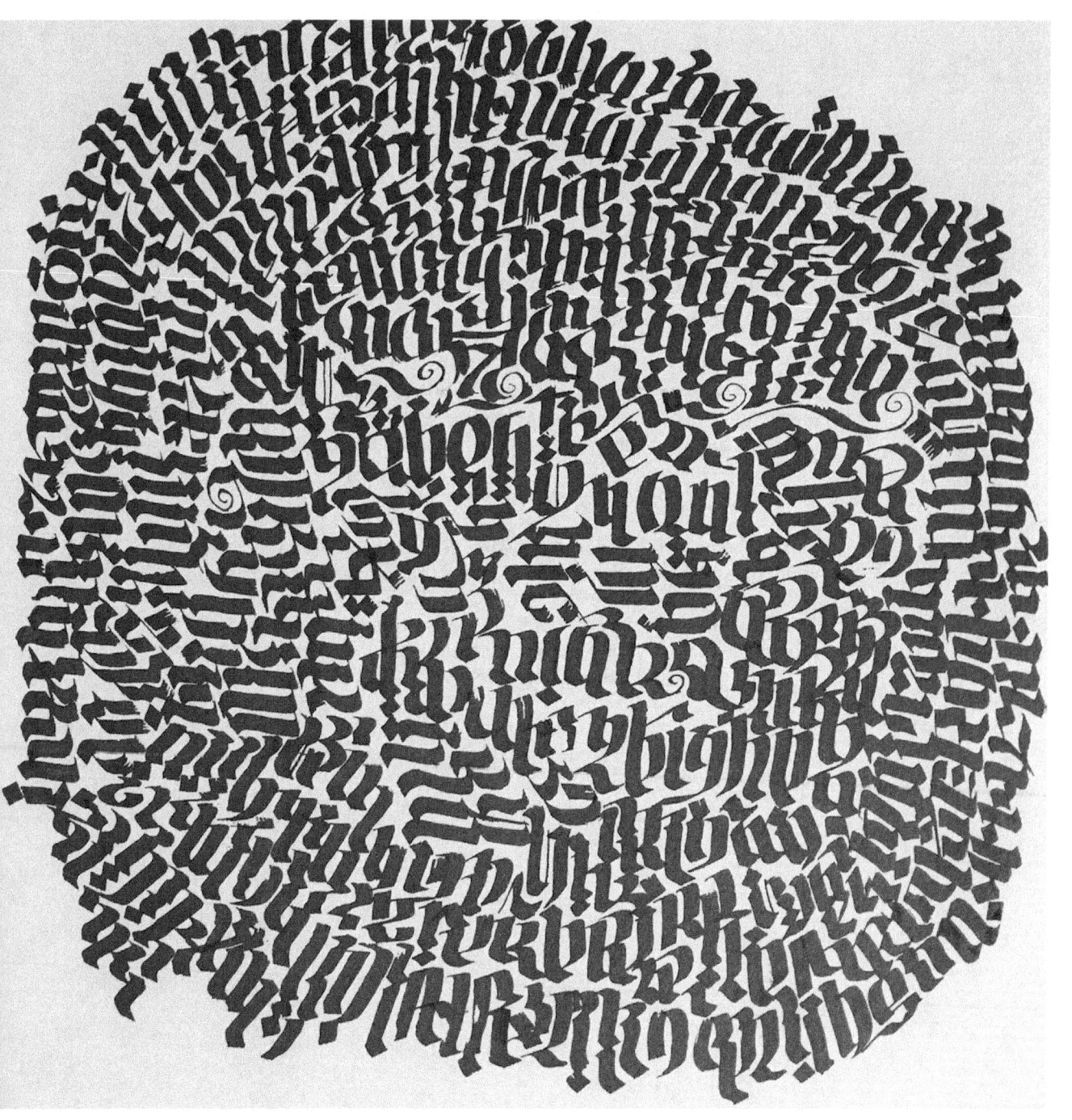

Strange horses on delicate legs, turn their impossible bodies
toward us. Close up, their eyes are astronaut helmets
gleaming but filled with my reflection, myself an alien landscape.

I am a distant creature, barren and dangerous.

Scrape the hair of the deer to draw the deer from the cavewall. Sharpen
your cooled cinder with an edge of stone, draw a map out, of here.

The edge of the map is only where the legs were, the tail, the heart. Wrap the
drawn skin around your shoulders and use it to be still through the tide of
thousand crumbling cities, wall by wall.

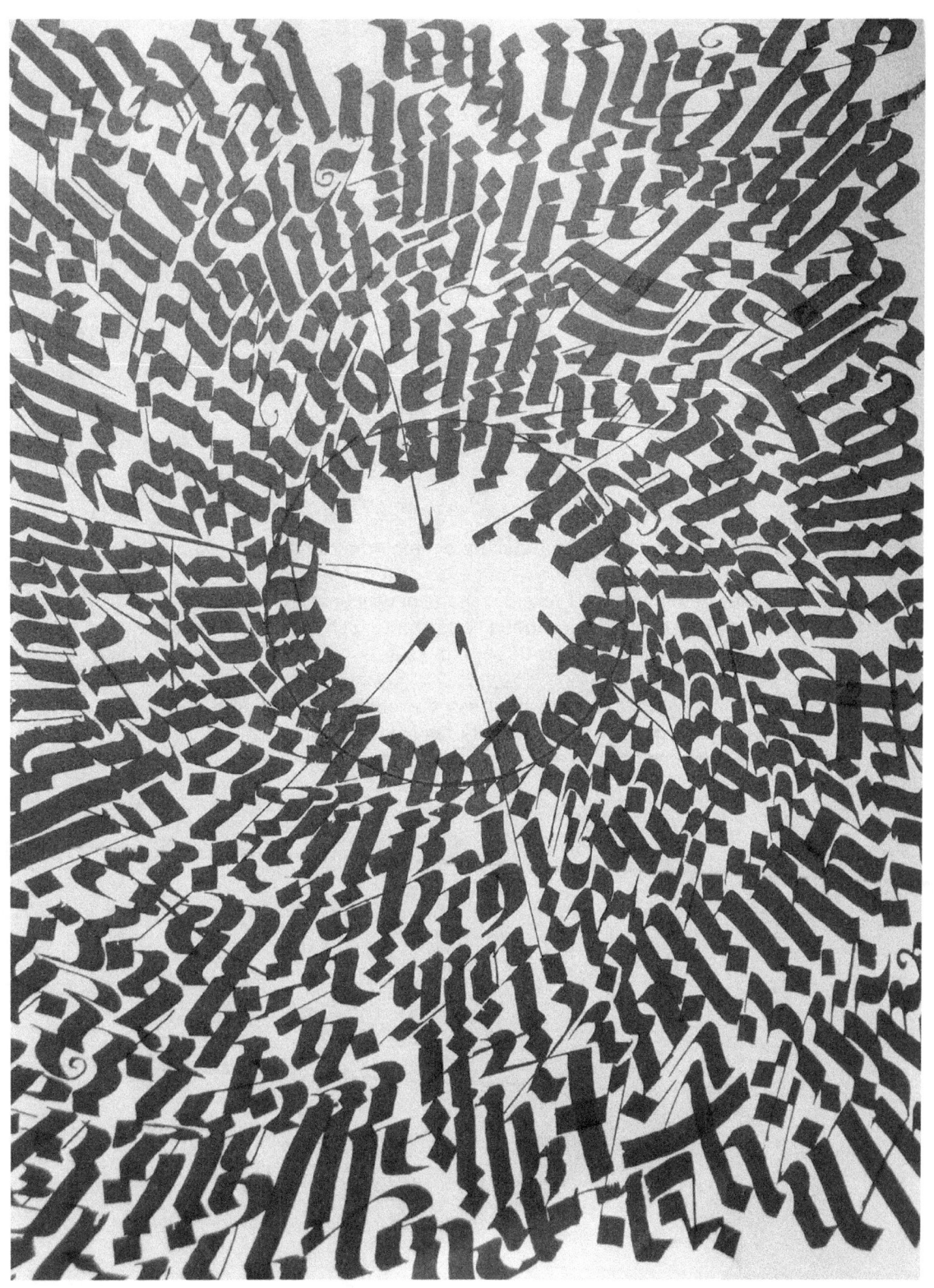

Some stones fit the hand, some are dimpled by the thumb of water.

Some of them want to take the shape of welcome,
shadowed convex of a cupped hand, pouring shade over the eyes
in order to see a distance through the sun.

I don't want to read it, enchantress, ancient horses straining
to pull the magnificent rocks out of my bloated eyes,
thier tongues frothing, everything poised to spill.

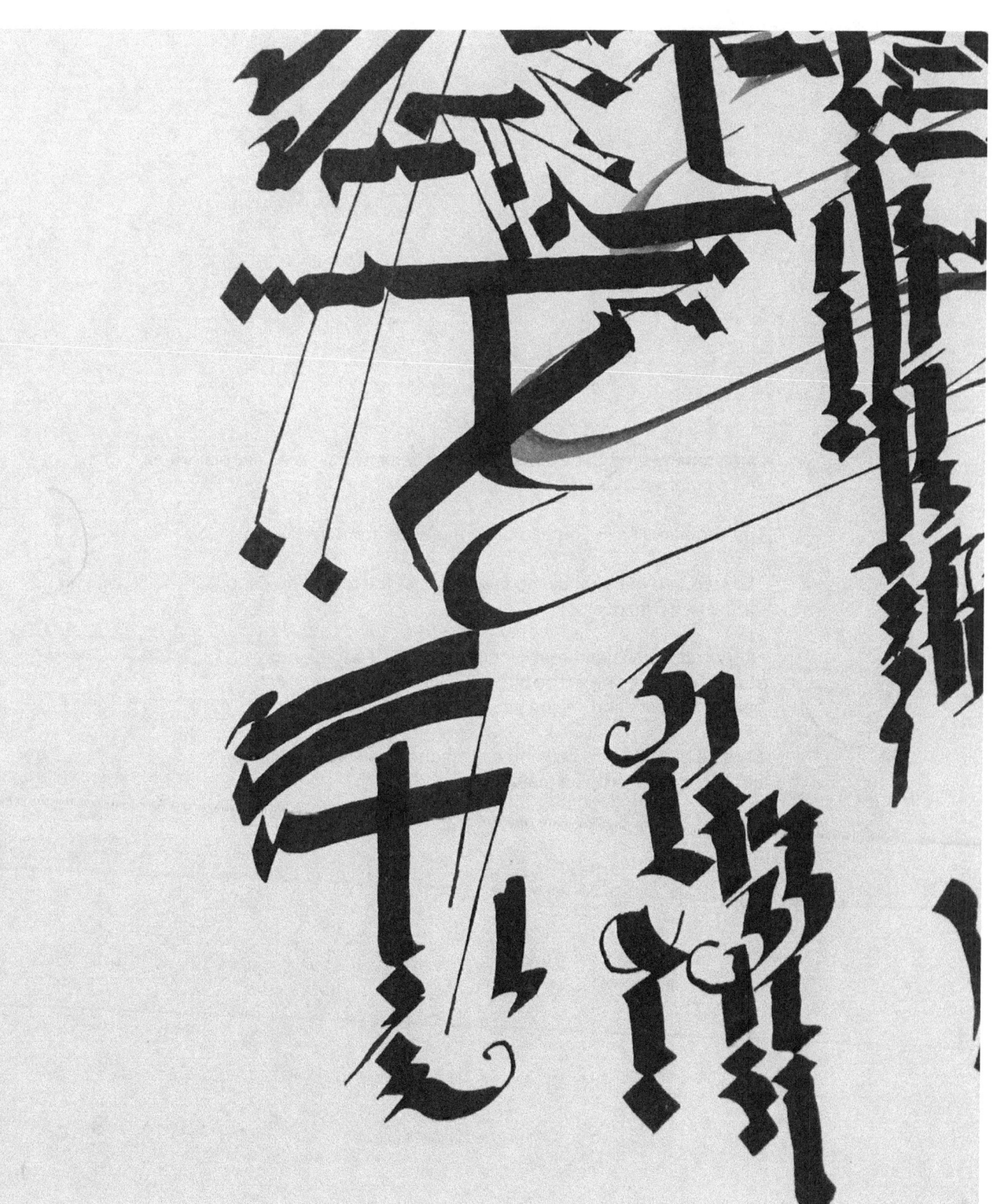

I am embarrassed to be naked, even under water where I am distorted
and comforted by touch.

The engineers have come to drain the water from the quarry.

They will find me a thousand feet down, at the toe of the deep, dark sock, waiting
for the performance of light.

Hurry your weaving, throat-cloud, a thousand beginnings
stutter to shard. The entire bib of my life is shale,
barbed to years and slicing your honeyed feet.

My soul is bitten, you call and call among the waste
but I am only shards beneath you.

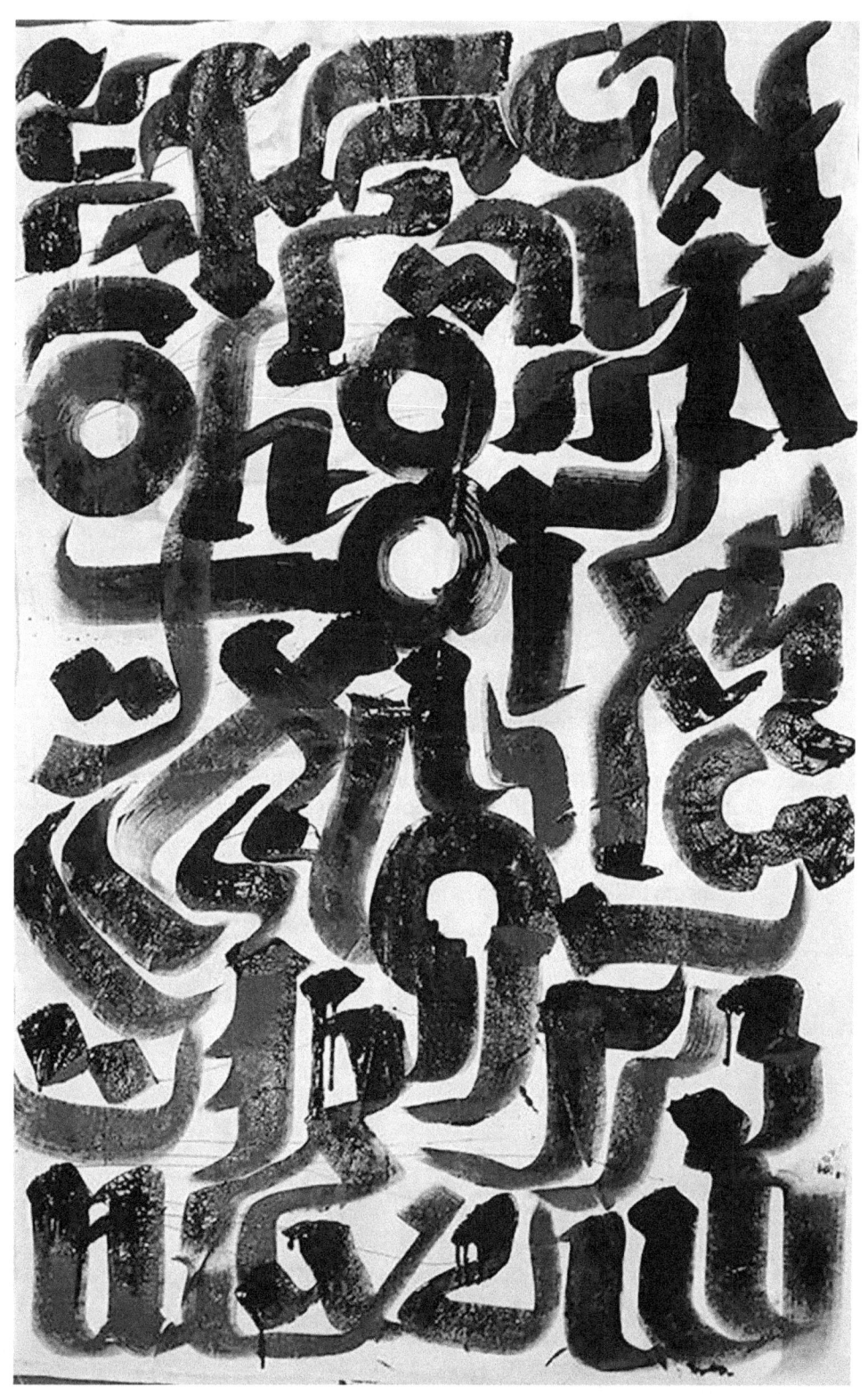

Hold this up as a memory, like a room,
like a box in which a stone is laid.

The box is portable and cardboard and fits in your pocket.
It might carry a gift, or a tiny pair of scissors.

It might carry a valuable promise the way a wall carries the roof,
or an upper floor where your lover paces desperately against the night.

Accent of your scent, the earth around the tulip bulb,
plucked from soft dark ground, rubbed upon my cheek
leaves a mark, dominion, suffering the hollow,
the adornment of water is the curve it makes
as it meets the dirt and pushes into the dance.

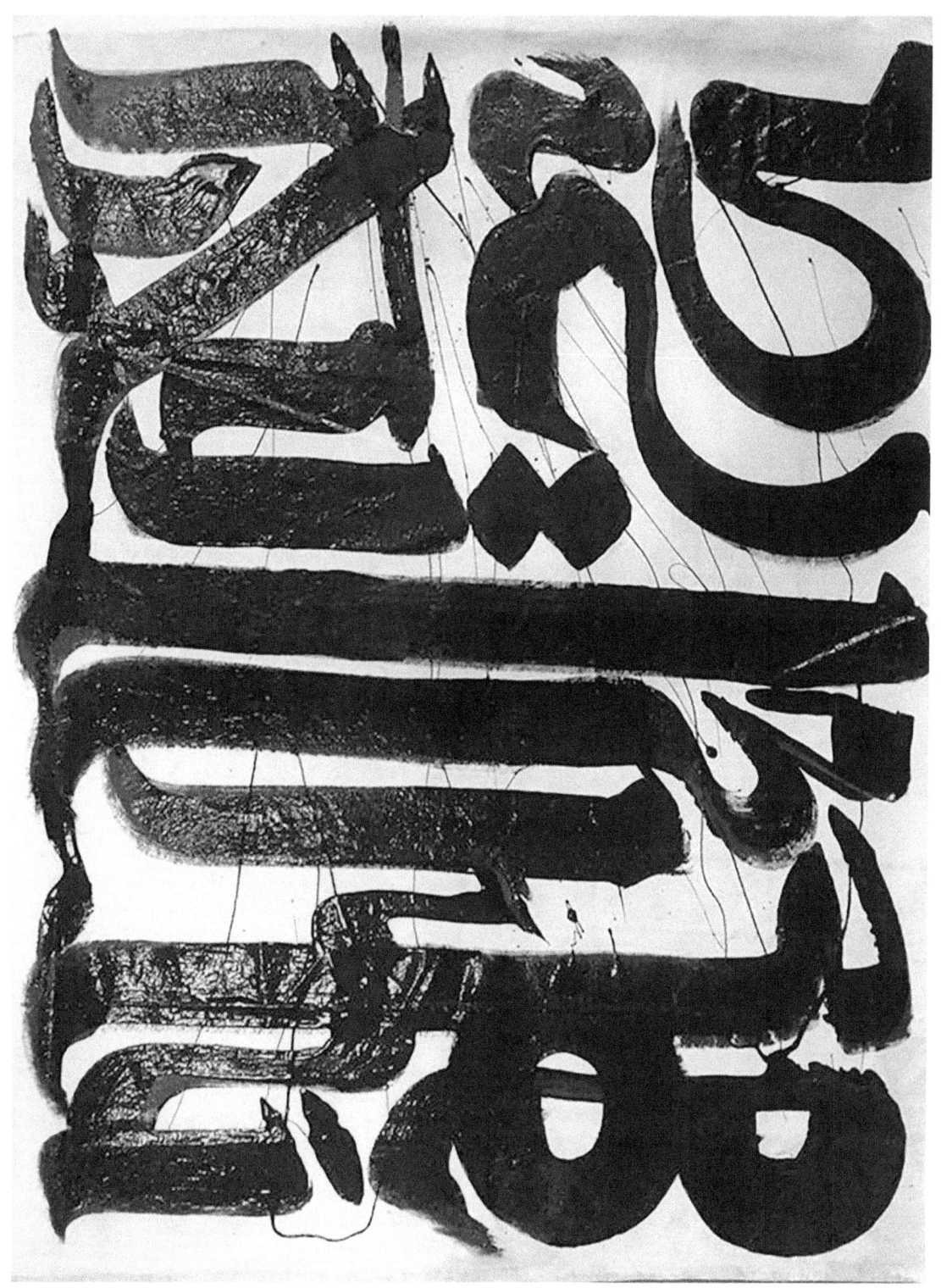

O canyon, decayed mountains in tidy arrangement, O how to be swallowed by a landscape
Now jagged shutters, tidal basins, outcroppings of god in an ocean of skin, so much
caressing water soaking through me, down to my water-table. I'm rising.

Living dead word, vanity of spring and flowers.
Immortal air, immortal stone, my love is frozen between them,
honey and wax in winter, golden and moon heavy.
I suffer, cruel to the skin, scarred at the waist
like the horizon swallowing the moon, breaking dark.

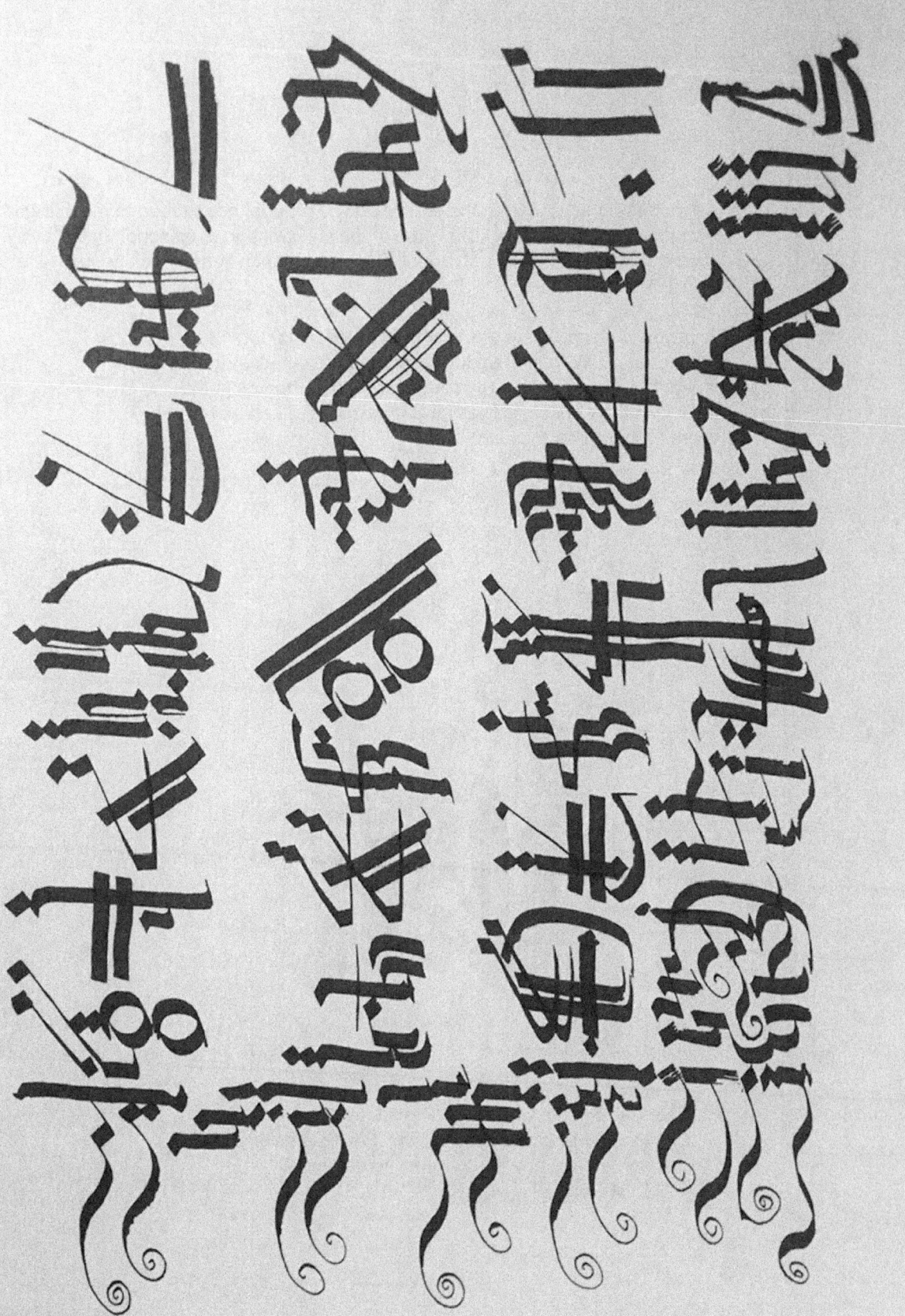

The moon is split rock from the earth's body. Perhaps they rubbed to much together and became fractioned out, the torso of the sun twisting in disappointment away, casting an arm of shielding shrapnel. There is so much light in a diamond I have to keep it in a box.

I love you in sleep. There are not tears in sleep. No pursuit
or penetrating. Words lift up to the fan and are cut away, groups
of people disperse, going to make their reports, horses graze
and shake their heads, lazy as forgotten violins. Sleep
where nothing is in ambush.

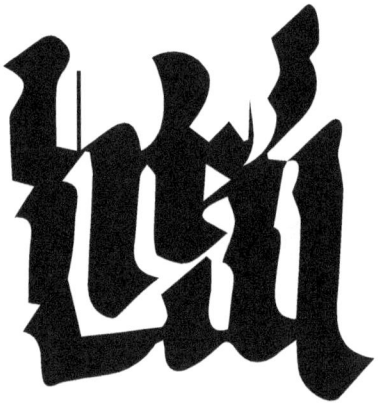

Hesitate through the branches, these lines cut.
　　　Innocent stones, cut the lines. Power lines electric
　　　something, power structure, something.
　　　Dewdrops.

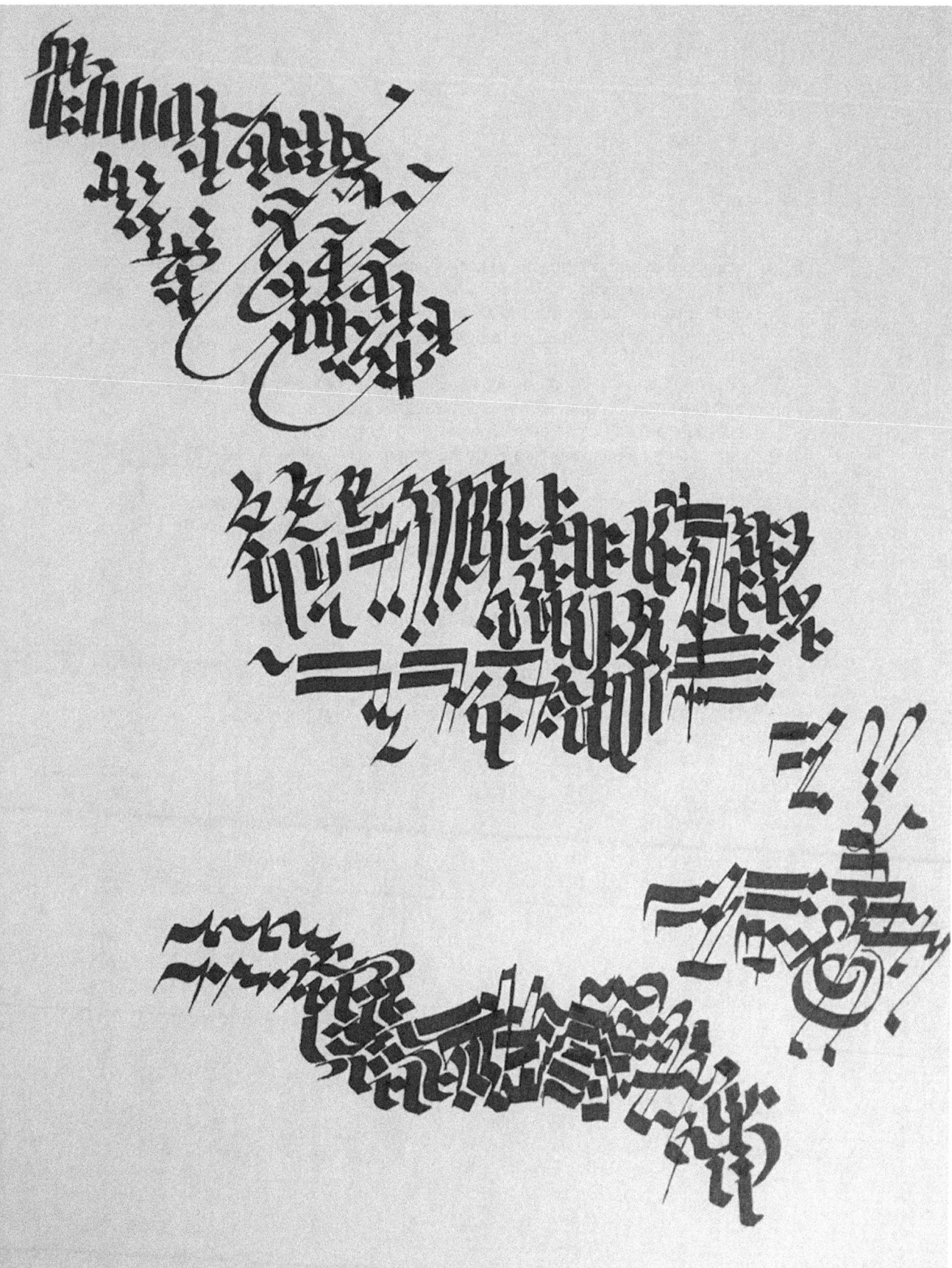

I can't get over the high wall of pure syntax to get in to your garden.
The hills are stripping down and I can see everything
up to the pure mountains, the swaths of dark growth,
balustrades of trees, the river's hygienic twist to hip,

but I can't grip the ivy, it comes away in powder, crushed pills
drift like snow, eroding icebergs. There is the wall,
but there are no firm streets. Only swirling dark binaries,
purchasing one another like butterfly wings.

Fulcrum of speech, blotting the pointed wound with my rag,
the needle on the compass points to fish, points to moon,
the magnetic class of water in which sad light
tiny larvae swim.

It's not a joke. Concentric strata, stone eyes of the blind statue,
imperfect struggling hands
lifting an astronomical heart, crenelated engine, like a star making a fist.

The sun's death diffuses, then compresses into my stone,
my needle, holding up your hair
                              with its bright tip.

-

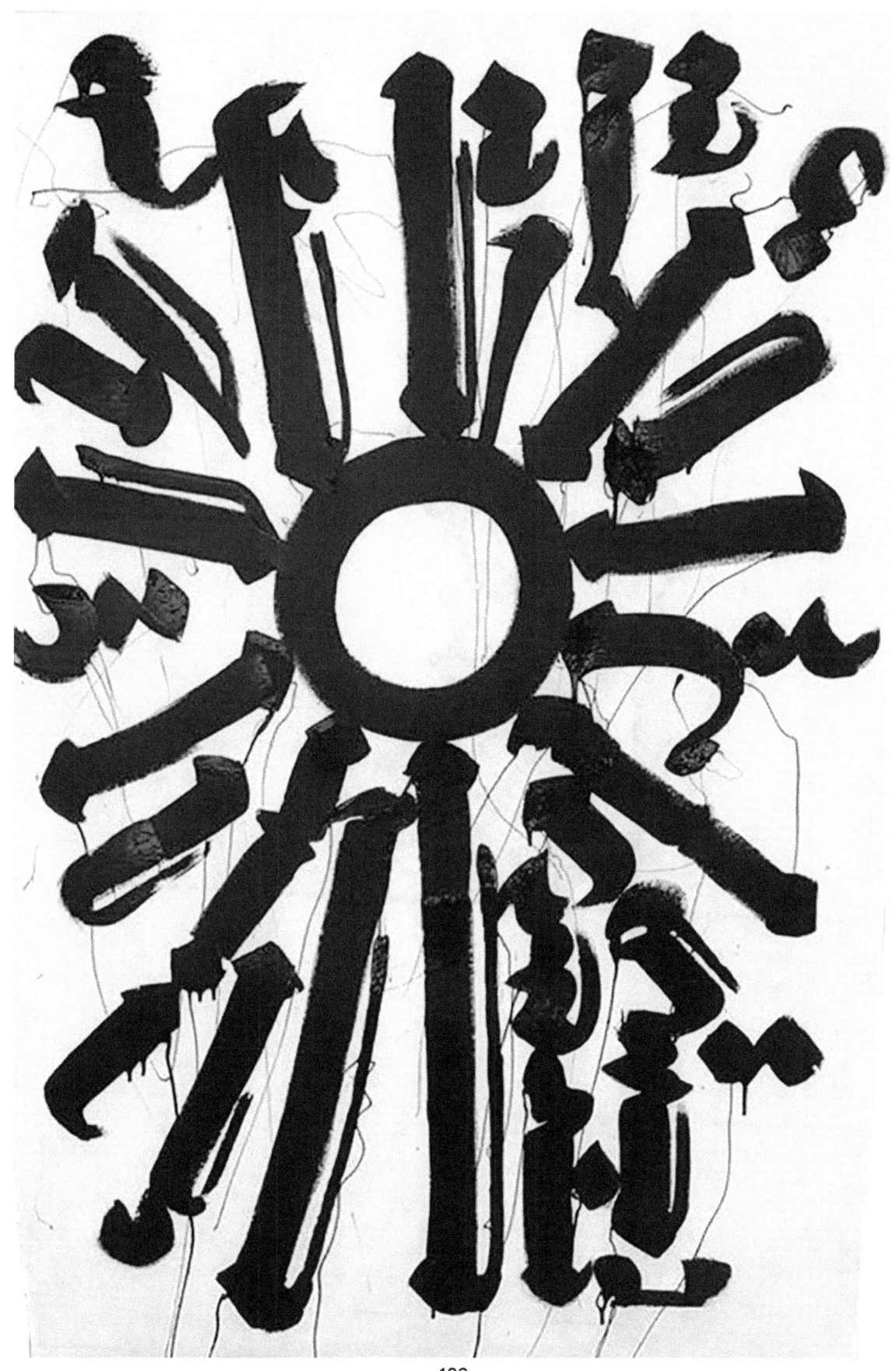

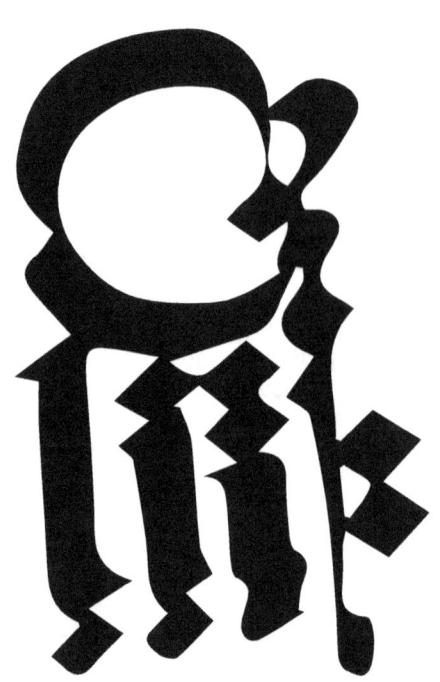

www.ingramcontent.com/pod-product-compliance
Lightning Source LLC
Chambersburg PA
CBHW080619190526
45169CB00009B/3240